Soup with Fresh Basil Butter • Garlic Soup with Chick Ice

and Smoked Salmon Bisque • Thick Fennel Soup with Spinach Pastina • Re

Bacon Crisps • Caldo-Verde: Kale, Potato, and Chorizo Soup • Roasted Beet an

Dil • Zucchini Foam with Crab • Parmesan Crisps • Lemon-Poppy WafersSix Dips f

d Eggplant "Ketchup" • Yogurt-Tahini • Goat Cheese-Cilantro • Cucumber-Scallion

Mignonette • Smoked Salmon with Wasabi Cream • Jean-Georges' Leek Terrine wi

cini and Tomato Frappé • Jumbo Shrimp on the Half-Shell, "8-Vegetable" Granita

amy Feta Dressing • "Lamb's-Quarters" Lettuce and Pear Salad, Stilton Dressing

• 1-2-3 Tomato Salad with Ricotta Salata and Dill • Endive Leaves and "Endiv

atoes and Basil • Poached Salmon, Cilantro-Yogurt Sauce • Julienned Beefstea

moked Salmon, Cucumbers Pressé • Parmesan-Crusted Asparagus, Poache

ennel and Grape Tomato Salad, Tomato Dressing • Sautéed Shrimp in Cor

ked Fennel Parmigiana • Whole-Wheat Linguine in the Style of Sardinia

ni-Garlic Sauce • Steamed Mussels al Finocchio, Toasted Fennel Fronds

th Rosemary • Lacquered Salmon, Pineapple-Soy Reduction • Bay-Steame

Corn, Chipotle "Cream" • Pepper-Seared Mahi Mahi, Mango Salsa • Bake

age • Salmon Demi-Cuit, Sauce Moutarde • Bluefish under a Brick, Whol

d Sea Bass, Parsley-Garlic Sauce • Layered Flounder and Smoked Salmon

hese-Style • Next Wave Tuna Salad: Tartare and Seared • Lemon-Thyme Roa

e-Strength Sherry Consommé • Cold Poached Chicken, Avocado and Mang

ven-Dried Grapes • Chicken Chaud-Froid with Yogurt-Lime Glaze • Red Her

hini Coulis • Rolled and Tied Turkey Roast with Fresh Sage and Baked Pea

ork Loin with Orange-Chipotle Jus • Pork Tenderloin with Sweet Mustard an

th Apricots • Lamb Chops Provençal • Rib-Eye Roast, Gravlax-Style • Boeuf à

Chilled Spring Pea Soup • Cauliflower Vichyssoise with Chive Cream • Sou

healthy 1

2

3

healthy 1 2 3

fat-free ◆ low fat ◆ low calorie

THE ULTIMATE THREE-INGREDIENT COOKBOOK

ROZANNE GOLD

PHOTOGRAPHS BY ANITA CALERO

Foreword by Dr. Barbara Levine, RD, PhD
Co-Director, Human Nutrition Program, The Rockefeller University;
Director, Nutrition Information Center, New York Hospital–Weill Medical
College of Cornell University

with Helen Kimmel, MS, RD, *Clinical Nutritionist*
and Dale Glasser Bellisfield, RN, CH, *Clinical Herbalist*

For Michael Whiteman, who nourishes me in every way

Published in 2001 by
Stewart, Tabori & Chang
A division of Harry N. Abrams, Inc.
115 West 18th Street
New York, NY 10011

Library of Congress Cataloging-in-Publication Data
Gold, Rozanne, 1954–
     Healthy 1-2-3 : the ultimate three-ingredient cookbook / by Rozanne Gold ;
     photographs by Anita Calero; foreword by Barbara Levine, with Helen Kimmel
     and Dale Glasser Bellisfield.
          p. cm.
     Includes index.
     ISBN 1-58479-040-7
     1. Low-calorie diet—Recipes. 2. Low-fat diet—Recipes. I. Title.

RM237.73 .G655 2000
641.5'635—dc21   00–029179

Designed by Amanda Wilson
Food Stylist: Margarette Adams
Prop Stylist: Barbara Fierros

Printed in Italy

10 9 8 7 6 5 4 3 2 1

First Printing

BOOKS BY ROZANNE GOLD

Little Meals: A Great New Way to Eat and Cook

Recipes 1-2-3: Fabulous Food Using Only 3 Ingredients

Recipes 1-2-3 Menu Cookbook

Entertaining 1-2-3

contents

foreword
by Dr. Barbara Levine

We take out, we order in, we open cans and microwave pre-packaged meals made from we know not what. We are a nation obsessed with nutrition and slimness, but in our efforts to attain these goals, we consume huge amounts of sugar-free foods containing things that may well be more dangerous than sugar and fat. We follow one-dimensional diets—one week bacon-cheeseburgers, the next week grapefruit—and somehow wind up even fatter. And all the while, we increasingly distance ourselves from the goodness of whole foods, from the hallowed craft of cooking, and from the unmatchable pleasures of sitting around the dinner table enjoying a good meal.

Clearly, help is needed. But all too often those who would offer it are scientists who view food as the sum of its nutritional components. And the diets they prescribe, while healthy, aren't the kind of regimes to which one can happily adhere for a week, let alone a lifetime.

What we need is more people like Rozanne Gold. First and foremost a chef, Ms. Gold has, over the course of her twenty-year career, made an unshakable commitment to identifying the finest recipes and then simplifying them in her trademark manner so that extraneous elements fall away and the essential deliciousness shines through. Less well known is that Ms. Gold has herself struggled with serious weight issues and has emerged as one of the sveltest people on the food scene.

Resolutely anti-fad, Ms. Gold adheres strenuously to moderation. In her kitchen, there are no "off-limits" foods. Indeed, one of the keys to achieving truly moder-

ate food intake is to be satisfied, even delighted, with what one is eating. And who is going to be satisfied with a regimen that eschews butter, oils, cheese, and sugar? Humans have cherished these foods for millennia; Ms. Gold shows us how to enjoy them while keeping calories and fat grams within sensible limits.

Ms. Gold is so adamant in her pledge never to compromise on taste and style, you may be surprised to learn how nutritionally sound this book is. In fact, she worked closely with both a nutritionist and a clinical herbalist to produce this collection of recipes, each of which fits into one or more healthful category: fat-free, low fat, or low calorie. All the recipes in **Healthy 1-2-3** are grounded in the latest nutritional research. In the last decade, knowledge of the workings of physiologically active compounds in food has changed the role of diet in health. Specifically, the antioxidants found in many fruits and vegetables have been shown convincingly to protect the body against disease and to help boost immunity. Researchers continue to discover ways to isolate and target the health-enhancing properties of the foods that contain them. Accordingly, Ms. Gold builds her repertoire around such nutritional "stars" as garlic, grapes, olive oil, berries, oily fish, cruciferous vegetables, legumes, and green tea.

Healthy 1-2-3 is above all suffused with Rozanne Gold's manifest joy in taking high-quality foods and enhancing them through the artistry of cooking, and with her belief that eating well means enjoying foods that are good for the body as well as for the soul.

introduction

The power of **Healthy 1-2-3** is its simplicity.

Every recipe uses *only three ingredients* (not including salt, pepper, and water). And each recipe clicks into one or more easy-to-understand categories: fat-free, low fat, and low calorie. It is a cookbook with a mission, demonstrating how to include everything—from caviar to chocolate—in a deliciously healthy diet.

In this book, to eat healthfully means eating a combination of foods low in calories and/or fat (over half my recipes fall into both categories); eating foods that are inherently good for you by dramatically upping your intake of fruits and vegetables; eating a broad array of foods for maximum benefit; avoiding processed foods whenever possible; balancing overindulgence with restraint; and most of all, learning to appreciate fresh, simple cooking.

Limiting recipes to three ingredients is the easiest way I know to cook, and eat, in a healthy way. My objective is to provide a repertoire of dishes that maximize flavor by removing extraneous ingredients and by reducing calories and fat, which is what most of us should care about.

Collectively, these recipes represent a remarkably liberating way to restore your body's nutritional equilibrium, to maintain your weight, or to rediscover your waistline. We are bombarded with complex and conflicting dietary information that requires elaborate skills to make sense of it all. Seduced by fads that banish entire food groups, we overcompensate by gorging on unbalanced diets; seduced by fat-free processed foods, we consume double and triple portions; seduced by canned nutri-shake meals, we use them as snacks instead. We are a society obsessed with healthy eating, yet Americans get more obese year by year.

The simple truth is that we're doing it all wrong. "Calories are the only thing that matter in weight management," says Dr. Marion Nestle, chairman of New York University's Department of Nutrition and Food Studies, "and no diet has yet defeated the law of thermodynamics. All calories, no matter what food source they come from, are metabolized to produce your body's energy. If you consume more calories than you use, you'll gain weight. If you take in fewer calories than you use, you'll lose weight. As for fat," says Dr. Nestle, "too much saturated fat can clog your arteries."

So, **Healthy 1-2-3** addresses everyone's desire to eat better without requiring a degree in advanced mathematics or nutrition; it concerns itself only with the number of calories and the amount of fat in each recipe.

Polenta Tart with Melted Tomatoes and Smoked Mozzarella (page 68)

◆ **Fat-free** means less than one gram of fat per serving.
◆ **Low fat** means fewer than 5 grams of fat for soups, first courses, side dishes, restoratives, and desserts; and fewer than 10 grams for main courses.
◆ **Low calorie** means fewer than 165 calories for soups, first courses, side dishes, restoratives, and desserts; and fewer than 350 calories for main courses.

As well as olive oil, many recipes use such "forbidden" ingredients as butter, eggs, cheese, and cream, but still fit one of my healthful categories. Portions are ample and satisfying, adding to the appeal of this unique approach. Because it is one's overall diet that counts, I have assembled suggested menus in Chapter 7, "Healthy Menus with Wine."

These menus also fall into three easy-to-understand categories, entire meals that are: **very low in fat** (1 to 5 grams of fat and fewer than 675 calories); **very low in calories** (500 calories or fewer, with 30 percent or fewer calories from fat); and **low-fat, low-cal** (650 to 750 calories with 30 percent or fewer calories from fat).

Or, selecting among the 200 recipes in this book, you can creatively compose meals as you see fit—entire dinners that are fat-free or dairy-free, vegetarian or kosher. You can select certain recipes because they are appropriate to the season or because you crave carotenes and lycopenes (natural compounds found in vegetables and fruits that may protect against disease). You may want to offset an afternoon binge with something more healthful that keeps you from overshooting your caloric objectives; or you may simply be seeking ways to cut fat from your family's diet without feeling punished.

It's as simple, and as healthy, as 1-2-3.

THE POWER OF THREE INGREDIENTS

My search for a simpler path through the complexities of cuisine and nutrition has led me to eliminate the excesses of "gastronomy" that have proliferated in recent years. By limiting each recipe to three ingredients, I've concentrated on vivid, unadulterated flavors that are both exciting and satisfying.

Many times I omitted fat to make room for a more healthful third ingredient. In its place, for example, there are wonderful fruit and vegetable reductions and herbs that add flavor and density. That is not to say that there's no place for fat here: Olive oil, rich in heart-healthy monounsaturated fat, is used often, as are small amounts of heavy cream, butter, and even bacon, in ways that add flavor without overloading recipes with calories and fat.

Great cooks know that the most important ingredient is the one you leave out. They scorn flavor cover-up and frivolous camouflage and know when *not* to be artful with a simple dish—and it is my belief that simplicity will amplify the impact of any dish because flavors are exponentially enhanced. Most foods are delicious in themselves: Their taste only has to be revealed.

A SHORT PERSONAL HISTORY As a kid

I morphed from a fat teenager into a plump adult. I hated my body and bemoaned my fate, for I was built exactly like my father (a professional fullback, no less) rather than like my svelte and glamorous mother.

I loved being home alone to raid the freezer, eating as much as I could (rearranging the rest so no one would notice) and feeling great satisfaction—until that familiar feeling of horror appeared at what I'd done, how awful I felt, how full I was, unable to sleep.

In those days I straightened my hair, parted it down the middle to cover most of my face, wore big glasses to hide the rest, and quietly wished I were dead.

After a trip to Europe when I was nineteen, I wanted to become a professional chef, but my academic upbringing catapulted me to graduate school in a field unlikely for a self-loathing body: human sexuality. I decided I liked food better.

I was thinner (but not much) and had yo-yo'd my way to anorexia and up again, when due to fortuitous circum-stances I became, at age twenty-three, the first official chef to the Mayor of New York.

Ed Koch and I both had an eating problem. No matter how much grapefruit juice I squeezed for him, and no matter how much black coffee I drank, there we were, two overweight New Yorkers roaming the halls of Gracie Mansion looking for a midnight snack.

After a whirlwind year with the mayor, I found myself in the demanding field of restaurant consulting, working in the world's finest restaurants. Glamorous, perhaps, but I again succumbed to the ruinous temptation of being around food all the time.

Life changed when Joe Baum, considered by many to be the greatest restaurateur of the century, called. I became culinary director of his firm (the Joseph Baum & Michael Whiteman Co.) and was consulting chef to New York's magical Rainbow Room, which the company owned and operated from 1985 to 1999. One of my responsi-bilities there was to develop "Evergreen," a low-calorie, low-fat dining concept for members of the Rockefeller Center Club who needed to eat smarter. In Evergreen, we succeeded in reversing health food's bad image by applying French techniques to a handful of superlative ingredients and cooking them perfectly. The result was a healthful, sophisticated cuisine marked by daring simplicity. I started losing weight.

I also discovered that hidden in this world of food and wine and all its pleasures was the concept of restraint. From Joe and his partners I learned to grasp the essence of a dish, to slowly savor small amounts of anything that was offered, and to demand the best of everything.

I learned to respect my hunger, and to anticipate the pleasure of satisfying it, but never to excess. My appetite felt better on the edge. I enjoyed everything more.

At that time, I began writing cookbooks about my new and simpler style. The first was *Little Meals,* based on smaller portions and bigger flavors, followed by *Recipes 1-2-3,* based on the paring down of ingredients to maxi-mize taste.

The former mayor and I, twenty-three years later, are now both as svelte as my mother, having separately found our own roads to caloric sanity.

In my book, sanity means liberation: not weighing myself every day and living within the limits of modera-tion. That's not always *daily* moderation, mind you, it's the theory of moderate averaging: if I overdo it one day, I "under-do" it the next. Even though I spend my life around food, I'm thin and fit and have maintained my weight for fourteen years by eating simply and following some important principles, which appear in the next section.

THE 1-2-3 DIET You can use this book to lose weight, to maintain your weight, or just to improve your diet—all in a nonradical, sustainable manner with simple, flavor-packed recipes.

If I need to lose weight, I hold my caloric intake to 1,400 calories a day and no more than 40 grams of fat—representing a diet with fewer than 30 percent of its calories from fat. You'll find fat and calorie figures on pages 214 to 216. At other times I'm much less doctrinaire. By using the labels given to each recipe you can effortlessly balance your diet with a variety of fat-free, low-fat, and low-calorie foods, with no sense of deprivation or compromise.

Knowing how to cook and eat in a healthful way is good for the body, enlightening for the mind, satisfying to one's sense of well-being. The following tenets have allowed me to trade self-consciousness for health-consciousness:

- ◆ Stop eating as soon as you feel satisfied, not satiated. This requires an honest dialogue between appetite and intellect, for you must re-learn what infants know instinctively: they turn away from the feeding spoon the moment they've had enough, while we tend to polish off our dinner plates and move on to dessert. Traditional wisdom says that our stomachs work best when 80 percent full, so respect the cues and push the food away.
- ◆ Don't eat when you're not hungry.
- ◆ Drink 6 to 8 large glasses of water daily. Between meals sip antioxidant green tea, since its bitter note can curb the appetite.
- ◆ Don't shop for food when you're hungry or you'll make indiscriminate choices.
- ◆ To maximize the pleasures of cooking, don't cook when you're full; it dulls the senses.
- ◆ Let your body rest a full twelve hours after dinner before eating again. If you finish at 9 p.m., eat again at 9 a.m.
- ◆ Learn the nutritional riches of the foods you eat.
- ◆ Buy the best and freshest ingredients.
- ◆ Eat lots of different things. One-dimensional diets are neither gastronomically nor nutritionally satisfying. "A balanced diet is the single most important factor in maintaining a healthy immune system," says Professor Simin Nibkin Meydani at Tufts University's Department of Nutrition and Immunology. A strong immune system protects against the common cold as well as cancer, it fights fever and fatigue, and promotes disease resistance and healing.
- ◆ Practice "moderate averaging" by balancing days of indulgence with days of "bearable lightness," during which you cut way back on your caloric intake. Sometimes I call this "measure your pleasure," which doesn't feel like deprivation but more like you're in control. Consider the wisdom of the philosopher Epicurus, who said, "Be moderate in order to taste the joys of life in abundance."

Mine is not the first 1-2-3 regimen. Omar Khayyám rhapsodized about "a loaf of bread, a jug of wine, and thou." Honoré de Balzac, the great nineteenth-century literary figure, had an eccentric diet of three foods: too much coffee, eggs, and fruit (indicative more of a particular lifestyle than a quest for health).

Sometimes I regress to Balzac's threesome when challenged by a blank manuscript page, but for most of us, a sensible diet is the best approach to healthy pleasures.

NUTRITIONAL FOUNDATION Helen Kimmel, a master of science–registered dietitian, has collaborated with me on three earlier cookbooks, *Recipes 1-2-3, Recipes 1-2-3 Menu Cookbook,* and *Entertaining 1-2-3,* expertly calculating my recipes' dietary values. Helen is president of Foodworks, Inc., a firm specializing in culinary and nutritional consulting.

Our streamlined approach to both the recipes and nutritional information in **Healthy 1-2-3** is unique—and fits today's lifestyles with ease. Helen has scrutinized and given her blessing to every recipe in this book, and has put them into simple categories, so that you are liberated from cumbersome number-crunching of fat grams, calories, and percentages. If you desire exact measures of calories and fat for individual recipes, they can be found on pages 212 to 214.

Calculations were based on a daily diet of 2,000 calories, using the most up-to-date databases, food labels, and resource books (such as *USDA Nutritive Value Books,* and the dietitian's bible, *Bowes' and Church's Food Values).*

While working on this book, Helen realized how opaque and misleading nutrition information can be. For example, sun-dried tomatoes packed in oil had fat and calorie counts that varied by 100 calories and 9 grams of fat per serving, depending upon the reference source. She bought several brands at my local supermarket and found some jars packed tight with tomatoes and little oil, and others with fewer tomatoes and lots of oil. Jars with more oil obviously were higher in fat and calories. To avoid miscounts such as this, Helen sampled a variety of products to derive average amounts of fat and calories.

A recipe must be read thoroughly before nutritional analysis can begin. Only edible portions actually consumed can count. For example, an ingredients list may call for two oranges, but the recipe may use one whole orange and only half the other; peels and trimming of fruit and vegetables have to be subtracted from total weight, and then analyses must be adjusted accordingly.

When marinades are used, only the amount actually absorbed by the food is calculated. When wine or other alcohol is cooked, most alcoholic calories evaporate. Helen also took into consideration my cooking techniques: if meat or poultry is broiled or grilled and the fat allowed to drain, calories and fat will be less than if the same item were braised or if some drippings were used.

The biggest challenge was to devise dishes that fit into my stringent criteria for fat and calories. Only the most delicious dishes survived.

But **Healthy 1-2-3** goes beyond the chemistry of just fat and calories, for it delves into nourishing the body as well as the psyche, and for this reason I also have collaborated with a clinical herbalist, who shares modern and ancient wisdom regarding what and how we eat.

FOOD AS MEDICINE Over two millennia ago, Hippocrates said, "Let your food be your medicine, and let your medicine be your food."

The notes preceding each recipe are based on intensive research, and guidance from nutritional experts and Dale Glasser Bellisfield, RN, CH. Dale is the clinical herbalist for the Kessler Institute for Rehabilitation and at Hackensack Medical Center's new Holistic Center for Health and Healing in New Jersey.

Dale notes that herbs and plants have distinguished curative histories dating back thousands of years, but only recently has the National Institutes of Health aggressively funded complementary and alternative medicine, hoping to find natural remedies for a multitude of ailments.

Ancient schools of medicine—such as the Chinese tradition and the Ayurvedic tradition in India—rarely distinguish between food and medicine, noting only the amount and duration of the intake, based on the needs of the "patient." Modern epidemiology shows how certain diets can protect you from, and possibly cure you of, such major afflictions as cancer, diabetes, stroke, and heart disease while other diets are implicated in causing them. The scientific community now is beginning to validate what older societies have known: that food is our first medicine.

Humans need more than forty nutrients: macronutrients (water, carbohydrates, proteins, lipids), which provide energy and regulate body heat; and micronutrients (vitamins and minerals), which help perform various metabolic functions. Nutritionists once reduced a food's value to just these critical components, but plants are complex entities with thousands of known and unknown substances that may have therapeutic or preventative functions, and so require further investigation.

There is convincing evidence that many foods play a big role in protecting against disease. Fruits and vegetables are loaded with protective phytochemicals and antioxidants. Phytochemicals are a huge group of biologically active substances found only in plants that can bolster our defenses against disease. Antioxidants are compounds found in food that can protect our cells from oxidative damage, caused by unstable molecules called free radicals, that results from normal metabolism and environmental factors. Minerals that support antioxidant efforts are iron, zinc, and selenium, which can be found in meat, grains, and nuts, in addition to produce.

As research and experience expand, specific foods appear to have significant positive impact upon our health. For example, the intake of cruciferous vegetables (broccoli, cauliflower, cabbage, turnips, kale, bok choy) is associated with low rates of several cancers in humans. So eat lots of them. You'll find many recipes included here.

Fresh fruits contain many protective phytochemicals that act as antioxidants, scavenge carcinogens, and stimulate the immune system, so increase your daily intake. You'll find over 30 such recipes here.

Sautéed Chicken Breast with Oven-Dried Grapes (page 90)

Alliums, the family of garlic, onions, chives, and shallots, have well-documented health attributes and you'll find these incorporated, in great measure, here.

Herbs and spices also contain phytochemicals, and their medicinal use is growing rapidly among those seeking more natural remedies. You'll find many recipes using interesting herbs and spices here.

Olive oil contains protective polyphenols and cholesterol-reducing properties that may protect the heart, and you'll find it used, predominantly, here.

No longer able to separate nutrition from medicine, the scientific community has opened its doors to the new (or very old) field of alternative medicine. So you'll find recipe headnotes linking the two here.

"So eat well," says Dale, trained in Eastern and Western medicine. "Eat lots of colors, eat variety, eat your family's ancestral foods, eat with a peaceful heart, eat when you're hungry, eat in moderation, eat unprocessed food, eat in gratitude for what it has taken to get food to your table. Food, especially with laughter, is our best medicine."

FOOD AND WINE TOGETHER

Hippocrates, "the father of medicine" 2,450 years ago, recommended wine as part of a healthy diet, but a decade ago the nutrition police and government backed moralists were doing an effective job of tamping down wine consumption in this country.

Then came the French Paradox, a revelation that Gaulois-smoking, exercise-deprived citizens of France who luxuriated in foie gras and Roquefort cheese lived longer than diet-obsessed Americans—and had far lower rates of heart disease.

The key was their consumption of wine, and more specifically, red wine. The conclusion, since demonstrated by numerous studies, is that people who drink regularly and in moderation live longer, are less likely to die of strokes, and stay remarkably healthier than those who avoid alcohol altogether: they suffer about 20 percent fewer heart attacks or deaths from stroke, according to the American Heart Association.

Wine, of course, is no more a universal curative than garlic or broccoli, but two glasses a day (less for women) relaxes blood vessels, protects against clotting, and enhances the "good" cholesterol. Among its myriad compounds are polyphenols, naturally occurring plant chemicals that seem to reduce the risk of heart disease and some kinds of cancer. Since most of grapes' phenols are in their skins, and since white wines are made with minimal skin contact, the health focus has been on red wine.

Recent research suggests that other components in wine increase mental activity and ward off dementia and Alzheimer's disease in older people. In the land of continuous improvement, the Japanese are now adding blueberry juice (for better eyesight) and polyphenols to their wines.

But this book is about healthy eating and not about biochemistry, so perhaps a more important point should be made: a major health benefit of wine may come from the very act of drinking it, because it induces us to pause and to relax, and because it enhances the overall experience of a meal. And that is why we toast, "To your health."

THE ESSENTIALS

Please read each recipe before shopping. Measure or weigh everything carefully. I do not encourage substitution of ingredients, since the three-ingredient balance of flavors has been harmonized like a musical chord. In addition, the nutritional analyses are based on the precise ingredients, measurements, and techniques found in each recipe.

SALT-PEPPER-WATER As in my three preceding 1-2-3 cookbooks, salt, pepper, and water are "free ingredients" because they are essentials in all cooking.

- **Salt:** I use kosher salt for regular cooking, as do most chefs. In some recipes I specify fine or coarse sea salt because their flavors are more complex. Occasionally I call for *sel gris* or *fleur de sel,* expensive salts from France that give dishes great style and crunch, especially when added at the end. Salt orchestrates flavor by enlivening and integrating the tastes of other ingredients. If you have high blood pressure, are on a sodium-restricted diet, or if you retain lots of water, modify my suggestions as you wish.

- **Pepper:** Use white or black peppercorns freshly milled in a pepper grinder that adjusts from fine to coarse, or crush peppercorns with the flat side of a knife when very coarse mignonette pepper is required. Cracked or butcher-grind black pepper is sold in jars, but at a loss of bouquet.

- **Water:** I use tap water, but you may use filtered or bottled water as your environment dictates. Use water as a base in soups (unlike stocks, it won't cover up the elemental tastes in these simple recipes) and to deglaze pans to extract every last bit of a recipe's flavor.

INGREDIENTS "I only want the best so I can critique all the rest," says my husband about a variety of subjects. When it comes to ingredients, he's got it right—because

Pink Grapefruit in Guava Nectar (page 178)

my recipes are about their ingredients. So you must be willing to trade up a bit, to journey to a farmer's market, to use all your senses in selecting the best of what is required. Inferior products undo the very essence of these recipes.

Judge a vegetable by its color. Broccoli, for example, that's tinged with yellow is not as nutritious as one that's dark green; one that's limp has lost its nutritional and gastronomic reason for being; one whose buds have flowered is over the hill.

Try to eat in season and from your region, backyard, or even window box, when ingredients are at their healthy best.

Wherever possible use organic foods; they're free of pesticides and herbicides, hormones, and antibiotics, and no one's tinkered recently with their DNA. Health risks aside, organic food usually tastes better. Years past, this was not the case, because organic produce lay lifeless on grocers' shelves for too long, but today's supply bursts with vitality, reflecting renewed passion among regional farmers and increased consumer demand.

THE HEALTHY PANTRY The recipes in this book use fresh, natural, nutrient-rich ingredients, but do include, on occasion, some top-quality prepared products that make up a professional chef's larder.

These include flavored oils (garlic-, basil-, and lemon-flavored olive oils, roasted peanut oil, Thai-style curry oil, and truffle-flavored oil); shoyu (genuine fermented Japanese soy sauce); sun-dried tomatoes in olive oil; wasabi powder; terrific vinegars (from Spanish sherry vinegar to Japanese rice wine vinegar); exotic condiments like pomegranate molasses and tandoori paste; and a variety of aromatic honeys (from wildflower to buckwheat).

Some of these may be new to you, and are worth

discovering. Although the following ingredients can be purchased, these are pantry staples I make myself.

GARLIC OLIVE OIL
1 cup olive oil
8 large cloves garlic

Put oil in a small saucepan. Peel garlic and add to oil. Cook over medium heat until small bubbles form at the surface, and continue cooking for 5 minutes. Remove from heat and let sit for 2 hours. Strain through a sieve into a clean jar. Cover and refrigerate. Keeps for two weeks. *Makes 1 cup*

LEMON OLIVE OIL
1 cup olive oil
2 lemons

Place olive oil in a small saucepan. Grate rind of lemons to yield 1 tablespoon grated zest. Add to oil. Cook over medium-high heat for 2 minutes, or until tiny bubbles begin to appear and oil comes just to a boil. Stir often. Remove from heat. Add a pinch of kosher salt and stir. Let stand for 6 hours. Strain through a fine-mesh sieve into a clean jar. Cover and refrigerate. Keeps for two weeks. *Makes 1 cup*

PRESERVED LEMONS IN SALT
4 large organic lemons

Wash 2 lemons thoroughly and dry. Cut lemons into quarters, lengthwise, leaving them attached at the stem end. In a pint-sized jar with a tight-fitting lid, put a 1-inch layer of kosher salt and place cut lemons on top. Add enough kosher salt to completely cover lemons, so they sit snugly. Cut remaining lemons in half and squeeze to get about ⅓ cup juice. Pour juice over salt. Cover jar tightly. Refrigerate 2 weeks, shaking the jar daily to distribute liquid that will form in the jar. Tightly sealed, these will keep up to 6 months in the refrigerator.

Remove salt before using by running under cool water and patting dry. Use rind only. *Makes 8 wedges*

CINNAMON SUGAR
2 cups sugar
¼ cup ground cinnamon

Thoroughly mix sugar and cinnamon in a bowl. Cover tightly and store in a cool, dark place. Keeps indefinitely. *Makes 2 cups*

VANILLA SUGAR
2 cups sugar
1 long, pliable vanilla bean

Put sugar in a medium bowl. Split vanilla bean lengthwise. With tip of a knife, scrape out vanilla seeds, reserving split pod, and add seeds to sugar. Mix well with your fingertips, making sure seeds are well distributed (they are moist and tend to stick together). Stick split pod into sugar. Cover tightly and store in a dry place. Keeps indefinitely. *Makes 2 cups*

EQUIPMENT   I live in a simple kitchen: no microwave oven, no professional stoves or grills, no wood-burning or convection ovens.

I use a blender and a food processor, but not interchangeably, so please adhere to what my recipes specify. When pureeing hot liquids (which I do with lots of soups and sauces), cool them for at least 5 minutes before blending or processing. Otherwise they may erupt when hot air and steam build up.

I use a variety of heavy-duty 9-inch, 10-inch, and 12-inch nonstick skillets (which you find in good cookware shops and restaurant supply stores). If they come without covers, you may find glass ones sold separately at hardware stores.

Several of my recipes are steamed, so you will need a pot fitted with a perforated, flat-bottom insert (a combination you can find almost anywhere) or a covered bamboo steamer (sold in Asian markets) that fits comfortably on one of your present pots.

When steaming food in plastic wrap, it is imperative that you use a brand without the plasticizer DEHA, which may be an endocrine disrupter; you can obtain this information from Consumers Union or the manufacturers.

My favorite tool is my small jeweller's scale. Digital and easy to use, I weigh many of the ingredients in a recipe for accuracy. For larger amounts, or bulkier ingredients, I use a slightly larger, but still compact, scale with a separate hopper that will accommodate up to 10 pounds.

PRESENTATION   For ultimate satisfaction, I believe the look of a dish is as important as its taste, so in many recipes I give detailed serving instructions. Look at the photographs for inspiration. Here is where simple yet dramatic presentations can make dishes seem new again.

For when it comes to the senses, less is often more.

Chilled Spring Pea Soup • Cauliflower Vichyssoise v

Butter • Garlic Soup with Chicken and Cilantro • I

Ginger Essence • Yellow Split Pea and Smoked Salm

• Red Lentil Soup with Coconut Milk and Scallions •

Caldo Verde: Kale, Potato, and Chorizo Soup • Roasted

Roasted Tomato–Pepper Gazpacho, Basil Oil • Zucchini Fo

Chive Cream • Broccoli Soup with Fresh Basil

Cucumber-Spearmint Soup • Carrot Soup with

Bisque • Thick Fennel Soup with Spinach Pastina

weet Potato–Rutabaga Soup with Bacon Crisps •

et and Orange "Latte" • "Cream" of Swiss Chard •

with Crab • Parmesan Crisps • Lemon-Poppy Wafers

soups

Most soups are complicated affairs, chock-a-block with ingredients. These soups, on the other hand, rely not on a jumble of different flavors and textures, but on the perfect marriage of just a few tastes. Apart from a few heartier stewlike dishes, these soups tend to be silky, suave, and refined.

Lighter in texture and brightly colored with fresh vegetables and herbs, they deliver a wealth of vitamins and minerals. Even the filling, satisfying soups made with potatoes, pasta, and legumes are low in calories and fat.

I have two secrets to share about making simple, elegant, and healthful soups. First, the technique of pureeing the starchy ingredient with its cooking water adds great depth and richness, without the fat and calories that are a consequence (sometimes justified) of using cream in soups. Second, despite hundreds of years of culinary tradition, I've found that using stocks is not always necessary; stocks can mask the flavors of the few ingredients you choose to use.

Whether you call it gazpacho or potage, broth or bisque, if it's comfort you're after, double the portion and call it supper.

chilled spring pea soup

A flavor-packed marriage of sophistication and health, this delicate soup has a silken texture and Easter-egg color. In addition to signaling the end of winter, peas are a great source of dietary fiber. I use buttermilk because it brightens the flavor and is low in fat.

1 pound shelled fresh **peas** (about 4 cups), or use frozen peas

6 medium-large **shallots**

2⅓ cups **buttermilk**

Place fresh peas in a large saucepan with 3 cups cold water. Peel and finely chop shallots to yield ½ cup. Reserve 1 tablespoon chopped shallots for garnishing, and add remaining shallots to saucepan. Add ½ teaspoon kosher salt. Bring to a boil. Lower heat to medium and cook until tender and bright green, 10 to 15 minutes, depending on size of peas. Be careful not to overcook. If using frozen peas, thaw and add them to water, shallots, and salt mixture after 12 minutes of cooking, then continue to cook for 2 minutes.

Reserve 3 tablespoons cooked peas for garnish, placing them in a small bowl of cold water. Put remaining peas with cooking liquid in a blender. Puree until very smooth, gradually adding buttermilk. Blend until smooth. Transfer to a bowl and refrigerate for several hours, until very cold.

Strain soup through a coarse-mesh sieve. Add salt and freshly ground white pepper to taste. Serve in chilled soup cups or soup plates with a splash of buttermilk in the center. Sprinkle each serving with a few reserved peas and a bit of finely minced shallot.

Serves 6 (makes about 5¾ cups)

cauliflower vichyssoise with chive cream

low calorie & low fat

This cold soup, one of the most suave imaginable, is my low-calorie take on a traditionally high-fat French classic. Cauliflower, like broccoli and kale, is part of the mustard family and shares its brethren's beneficial phytochemicals, coumpounds that may help ward off certan diseases. In late spring and early summer, buy chives with their beautiful purple flowers attached to use as a garnish.

1 large head **cauliflower**, about 2½ pounds

1 large bunch **chives** with chive flowers attached

1 cup **half-and-half**

Trim base of cauliflower, removing leaves and any dark spots. Break into small florets. Place in a medium pot. Add 5 cups water and ½ teaspoon kosher salt. (Water will not cover cauliflower.) Cut enough chives into ½-inch lengths to get ⅓ cup and add to pot with cauliflower. (Reserve remaining chives.)

Bring to a boil, then lower heat, cover pot, and cook for 25 minutes, or until very soft. Transfer cauliflower and cooking water to a food processor. Process until ultra-smooth, gradually adding ⅔ cup half-and-half. You will need to do this in two batches. Transfer to a bowl. Add salt and freshly ground white pepper to taste. Let cool. Cover and refrigerate until very cold.

To make chive cream: Place ⅓ cup half-and-half, 2 tablespoons water, and a pinch of salt in a small saucepan. Chop enough chives to get ⅓ cup and add to saucepan. Bring to a boil. Lower heat and simmer for 1 minute. Transfer to blender and puree until very smooth. Let cool. Refrigerate until cold.

When ready to serve, taste soup, adding salt and white pepper if needed. Ladle cold soup into chilled bowls. Drizzle with chive cream. Break apart chive flowers, if available, and scatter petals over soup. Or, finely chop remaining chives and sprinkle on top.

Serves 8 (makes 7 cups)

broccoli soup with fresh basil butter

Here's a bowl of low-calorie comfort. Broccoli has appreciable amounts of calcium, vitamin C, fiber, folic acid, and thousands of phytochemicals to help protect against disease. Used in small amounts, butter adds voluptuous mouthfeel and great taste. Basil, an alluring herbal partner, is used two ways: as a flavoring agent for the broth, and in a stylish composed butter that floats atop the soup.

1 large bunch **broccoli,** about 1½ pounds

1 large bunch fresh **basil**

3½ tablespoons unsalted **butter**

Using a very sharp knife, cut a layer of the tiny buds from the head of the broccoli (about ⅟₁₆ inch off top) to yield ½ cup. Put buds in a fine-mesh sieve and lower the sieve into a pot of boiling water for 30 seconds. Then place sieve under cold running water to stop the cooking process. Set aside.

Using a vegetable peeler, peel broccoli stalks, removing all of the tough exterior. Cut off woody bottoms, and discard. Cut broccoli stalks and florets into ½-inch pieces. Place in a 2-quart pot.

Wash basil thoroughly and pat dry. Remove and reserve smallest leaves for garnish. Add ½ cup tightly packed basil leaves to broccoli. Cover broccoli and basil with 5 cups cold water and add ½ tablespoon kosher salt. Bring to a boil. Lower heat to medium, cover pot, and cook for 20 minutes until tender.

Place butter and ¼ cup packed basil leaves in bowl of a food processor. Add large pinch of kosher salt and process until just combined. Transfer to small bowl and refrigerate.

When broccoli is tender, transfer to a blender using a slotted spoon. Add the cooking water, reserving 2 cups. Process until very smooth, about 2 minutes, adding 2 tablespoons of the chilled basil butter in small bits while you process. You may need to do this in several batches. When very smooth, return to pot. Add salt and freshly ground black pepper to taste. Add additional cooking water from reserved 2 cups if too thick. Heat gently.

Ladle hot soup into soup bowls or cups. Sprinkle each serving with blanched broccoli buds, a thin slice of remaining basil butter, and small basil leaves.

Serves 6 (makes about 6 cups)

garlic soup with chicken and cilantro

This is chicken soup for both heart and soul. Garlic is purported to protect the heart by lowering blood pressure and cholesterol, and has been used therapeutically for thousands of years. Cilantro was once considered an aphrodisiac—and it could still be.

5 pounds **chicken wings**

1 large head **garlic**, about 3½ ounces

1 large bunch **cilantro**

Cut chicken wings in half, through the joint. Place in a 6-quart pot and add 10 cups cold water. Cut head of garlic in half horizontally and add to pot. Chop off cilantro stems, saving leaves for later, rinse, and add stems to pot. Add 1 tablespoon kosher salt and 1 teaspoon black peppercorns. Bring to a rapid boil. Lower heat to maintain a simmer, skimming foam from surface. Cover and simmer for 2 hours.

Strain soup through a fine-mesh sieve into a clean pot. Press down on solids to extract all juices. You will have about 10 cups broth. Reserve cooked chicken. Let broth and chicken cool, then refrigerate until cold.

Skim off all fat from cold broth. Heat just until boiling, lower heat to medium, and cook, uncovered, until reduced to 8 cups, about 30 minutes. (If stronger garlic flavor is desired, push another clove of garlic through a garlic press into soup. Simmer for 10 minutes longer.) Add salt to taste.

Meanwhile, pick off chicken meat from wings. Discard bones and skin. Place meat in a sieve and dip into hot broth to warm.

Place about ¼ cup warmed chicken in center of 8 shallow soup bowls. Tear reserved cilantro leaves and divide among soup bowls to taste. Pour 1 cup hot broth into each bowl.

Serves 8 (makes 8 cups)

iced cucumber-spearmint soup

Zen in a soup bowl: Cucumbers are cooling and diuretic to the body; yogurt is a good source of calcium and protein. My herbalist says that spearmint, when chewed, stimulates the brain, leading to better concentration and a sense of spiritual peace.

3 large **cucumbers**, about 1½ pounds

1½ cups plus 2 tablespoons plain low-fat **yogurt**

1 small bunch fresh **spearmint**

Peel cucumbers. Cut in half lengthwise and use a small spoon to scoop out seeds. Cut cucumbers into ½-inch chunks.

Place in blender. Add ½ cup cold water and 1 cup yogurt. Blend until smooth. Add ½ cup yogurt and 3 tablespoons coarsely chopped mint (or more if mint is mild). Add kosher salt and freshly ground black pepper to taste. Blend until very smooth.

Chill until very cold. (Place soup in freezer for 20 minutes before serving.)

Serve in large wine glasses or decorative mugs. Dollop with remaining yogurt and small mint sprigs.

Serves 4 (makes about 4 cups)

carrot soup with ginger essense

Devoutly simple, this vibrant soup is surprisingly low in calories even with the luxurious addition of heavy cream. Since most supermarket carrots taste lifeless, I try to use organic carrots for their better flavor. Ginger has a distinguished history as an anti-inflammatory and stomach soother.

2 pounds **carrots** plus green leafy carrot tops

5-inch piece fresh **ginger**

⅓ cup **heavy cream** plus 1½ tablespoons for garnish

Preheat oven to 400°F.

Wrap 2 peeled carrots in foil and bake for 1 hour, until soft. Let cool.

Meanwhile, trim remaining carrots, saving the carrot tops. Peel the carrots and cut into 1-inch pieces. Place carrots in a medium pot with 4½ cups water and 1½ teaspoons salt. Bring to a boil, lower heat, and cook, covered, for 35 minutes, or until carrots are very soft.

While carrots are cooking, prepare ginger juice: Peel ginger with a small sharp knife. Grate on large holes of a box grater. Place grated ginger in a paper towel and squeeze over small bowl to extract juice. You will have about 1½ tablespoons.

Transfer boiled carrots and cooking water to a food processor and process until smooth. Add ginger juice and ⅓ cup heavy cream and process until very smooth.

Return soup to pot. Add salt and freshly ground white pepper to taste, and a few tablespoons of water if soup is too thick. Heat gently.

Blanch 3 tablespoons carrot tops in salted boiling water for 1 minute. Refresh under cold water. Cut roasted carrots into julienne strips or into rounds. Ladle soup into soup bowls. Garnish with carrot julienne or rounds, a few blanched leaves from carrot tops, and a drizzle of remaining heavy cream.

Serves 6 (makes 5¾ cups)

yellow split pea and smoked salmon bisque

In this soup I've slyly substituted smoked salmon for the more traditional ham and it still results in a Scandinavian combination of flavors. Smoked salmon adds complexity as well as omega-3 fatty acids. Yellow peas provide soluble fiber and leeks impart sweetness to balance the slightly salty fish.

16 ounces dried **yellow split peas**

4 medium-large **leeks**, about 1¼ pounds

8 ounces sliced **smoked salmon**

Pick out any stones from peas. Place peas in a 4 quart pot with enough water to cover by 2 inches. Bring to a boil. Skim foam from surface and continue to boil for 2 minutes. Cover pot and remove from heat. Let sit for 1 hour.

Meanwhile, trim dark green part from leeks and set aside. Finely chop white and pale green parts only and wash thoroughly. You will need 4 heaping cups of leeks.

Drain peas in a colander and return to pot. Add chopped leeks, 6 ounces smoked salmon cut into small pieces, 5½ cups cold water, and ½ teaspoon kosher salt.

Bring to a boil. Lower heat to a simmer and cover pot. Cook for 30 minutes.

Meanwhile, cut dark green part of leeks into fine julienne to yield ½ cup. Wash well, and blanch in a small amount of boiling salted water until soft, about 3 minutes. Drain and refresh under cold water.

After 30 minutes, transfer contents of pot to a food processor. You may need to do this in several batches. Puree several minutes until very smooth. Add salt and freshly ground white pepper to taste. Serve immediately, garnished with blanched leeks and a small piece of remaining smoked salmon. If serving later, reheat soup, adding some cold water to thin.

Serves 8 (makes 8 cups)

thick fennel soup with spinach pastina

This is the sort of soup an Italian grandmother would make to soothe gastronomic disquiet. Fennel is a wonderful digestive aid, and red onion's antioxidants actually survive the long cooking process, while pasta, as every grandmother knows, is a good source of energy. The idea here is to puree these three ingredients into a singular comfort food with a smooth but palpable texture.

2 1-pound **fennel bulbs** with lots of fronds

2 large **red onions**

6 ounces **spinach pastina**

Wash fennel and pat dry. Cut the feathery fennel fronds from the bulbs, chop, and set aside.

Remove any brown spots from fennel bulbs and discard. Cut bulbs into ¼-inch dice. You will need 6 cups. Peel onions and finely dice. You will need 3 cups. Reserving ¼ cup onions for garnish, place diced fennel and onions in a large heavy pot. Add 8 cups water, ¼ cup chopped fennel fronds, and ½ tablespoon kosher salt. Bring to a boil. Lower heat to medium and cook, covered, for 40 minutes, or until fennel and onions are soft. Add pastina and cook, uncovered, over medium heat for 10 minutes.

Puree 4 cups of soup (with cooked pasta) in a food processor until smooth. Return to pot with remaining soup. Add kosher salt and freshly ground black pepper to taste. Cook for 10 minutes longer over low heat, stirring often. Soup will thicken. Serve immediately, garnished with chopped fennel fronds and reserved onion that has been finely minced. If serving later, add water to soup, as it will thicken as it sits.

Serves 8 (makes about 9 cups)

red lentil soup with coconut milk and scallions

Tiny red lentils, members of the legume family, are packed with nutrients disproportionate to their size. They're high in soluble fiber, protein, zinc, iron, and folic acid, benefiting overall health. Even with all that, this a very delicate potage.

1¾ cups red **lentils,** about 12 ounces

2 bunches **scallions**

⅔ cup light **coconut milk** plus 3 tablespoons for garnish

Rinse lentils in a fine-mesh sieve, discarding any pebbles. Place lentils in a medium pot.

Trim roots from scallions. Slice white and pale green parts thinly to yield 1 cup. Reserve dark green tops for garnish. Add sliced scallions to lentils with 5½ cups water and 2 teaspoons kosher salt.

Bring to a boil. Lower heat to maintain a simmer. Cover pot and cook for 20 minutes, or until lentils are very soft. Stir once or twice during cooking to prevent sticking.

Transfer to a food processor and process until very smooth. You may have to do this in two batches. Return contents to pot. Whisk in ⅔ cup coconut milk.

Add salt and freshly ground black pepper to taste. Heat gently before serving. If too thick, whisk in a little water.

Ladle into shallow soup bowls. Finely chop dark green scallion tops and scatter over soup. Drizzle each portion with ½ tablespoon coconut milk.

Serves 6 (makes about 6 cups)

sweet potato–rutabaga soup with bacon crisps

Sweet potatoes have even more beta-carotene than carrots. The body turns beta-carotene into vitamin A as it needs to. Rutabagas are a variety of turnip, also known as Swedes, with a waxy exterior and sweet yellow flesh. As for the bacon, well, it just tastes good. Use a nitrite-free brand, though.

2 large **sweet potatoes**, about 1½ pounds

1 large **rutabaga,** about 1½ pounds

5 slices **bacon**

Using a vegetable peeler, peel sweet potatoes. Cut in half lengthwise and then crosswise into ½-inch pieces. Peel rutabaga and cut into ½-inch pieces.

Cut 2 slices of bacon into ¼-inch pieces. Place in a 4-quart pot. Heat gently for a few minutes, until bacon fat is rendered, making sure bacon does not crisp. Add sweet potatoes and rutabaga. Using a large spoon, toss vegetables to coat with bacon fat. Cook over medium heat for 2 minutes.

Add 5 cups cold water, 1 teaspoon kosher salt, and 12 white peppercorns. Bring to a boil. Lower heat and cover. Cook 45 minutes, or until vegetables are very soft.

Meanwhile, in a large nonstick skillet, cook remaining 3 slices of bacon on each side until just crisp. Place crisped bacon on paper towels to drain.

Transfer vegetables and cooking liquid to a food processor. You will have to do this in 2 batches. Process until very smooth. Return to pot. Add salt to taste and heat gently.

Ladle soup into large shallow soup bowls. Crumble cooked bacon into small pieces and scatter on soup.

Serves 8 (makes 8 cups)

caldo verde: kale, potato, and chorizo soup

The Portuguese add lots of spicy sausage to flavor their classic soup, but this version doesn't tip the calorie scale. Kale provides generous doses of beta-carotene, calcium, fiber, and vitamin C; potatoes abound in potassium.

8 ounces **chorizo sausages**

4 large red or **Yukon Gold potatoes**, about 1½ pounds

1 large bunch fresh **kale,** about 1½ pounds

Prick two-thirds of the sausages several times with skewer. Reserve remaining sausages. In a large heavy pot put 2 quarts cold water and pricked chorizo sausages. Bring to a boil. Peel the potatoes and add to the pot. Lower heat to medium and cook potatoes for 30 minutes or until tender. Meanwhile, pick kale leaves from thick stems. Wash leaves in a colander. Drain well and cut leaves, using a very sharp knife, into fine shreds. You will have about 6 cups.

Remove chorizo from pot and set aside to cool. Using a potato masher, mash the potatoes in their cooking pot with the water so that only little chunks of potato remain. The broth will be thin.

Bring potato broth to a boil. Add kale and cook over medium heat for 10 minutes.

Meanwhile, slice the reserved uncooked chorizo into ¼-inch-thick slices. Cook in a nonstick skillet over high heat on each side until sausage is crisp and fat is rendered. Set aside.

Thinly slice boiled sausages and add to soup. Add fried sausage rounds and all pan juices. Simmer for 5 minutes longer. Taste the soup and add salt and freshly ground black pepper if desired.

Serves 8 (makes 8 cups)

roasted beet and orange "latte"

This intensely colored soup comes with a frothy head of steamed milk, which explains its name. Beets, perhaps because of their color, were traditionally eaten to build the blood and aid the liver, but in this soup I simply love the way their sweetness smacks up against the oranges' sunny acidity.

2 or 3 medium **beets** (no stalks or leaves), about 1 pound

4 medium juice **oranges**

1 cup low-fat (1%) **milk,** plus ¾ cup more for steaming

Preheat oven to 400°F.

Using a vegetable peeler or sharp knife, peel beets. Wrap beets in a loose pouch of foil and tightly seal at the top. Place in a pie tin or on a baking sheet. Roast for 1½ hours.

Wash oranges. Finely grate rind to yield 1 tablespoon zest. Cut oranges in half and squeeze to yield 1 cup juice. Set aside.

Remove beets from oven. Carefully open package to allow steam to escape. Cut beets into large chunks and place in bowl of food processor.

Process, gradually adding most of the orange juice. Continue to process, and add 1 cup milk. Blend until very smooth.

Transfer to large saucepan. Add kosher salt and freshly ground black pepper to taste. Add a little more orange juice if necessary. Add ½ tablespoon grated zest and heat gently.

Place hot soup in tall heatproof glasses or in large coffee cups. Steam ¾ cup milk using cappuccino steamer and evenly spoon frothy milk on top of each portion. If you don't have a steamer, simply scald milk in a small saucepan, whisking vigourously with a wire whisk, then spoon froth onto soup. Sprinkle with remaining orange zest.

Serves 4 (makes 3 cups soup plus steamed milk for topping)

"cream" of swiss chard

There's not a bit of cream in this ultra-creamy soup. When you puree potatoes and Swiss chard that have been cooked together, the result is pure silk. The dark, leafy greens provide lots of beta-carotene, potassium, and vitamin C, and potatoes chip in some of the B complex.

3 large **potatoes**, red or Yukon Gold, about 1¼ pounds

1 large bunch **Swiss chard**, about 1¼ pounds

2½ tablespoons unsalted **butter**

In a 4- to 6-quart pot, bring 8 cups water and ½ tablespoon kosher salt to a boil.

Peel potatoes. Halve the potatoes lengthwise and cut halves into ½-inch-thick slices. Add to boiling water. Lower heat to medium-high and cook, covered, for 20 minutes.

Meanwhile, wash Swiss chard thoroughly. Cut off bottom 3 inches of stems and reserve. Tear leaves into small pieces.

Add leaves to pot after potatoes have cooked for 20 minutes. Cook for 10 minutes longer. Do not overcook or chard will lose its bright green color.

Pour 3 cups cooking liquid from potato-chard mixture through a colander or coarse-mesh sieve. Set aside. Put potatoes, chard, and any remaining liquid in bowl of a food processor. Process until smooth. Add butter and process for several minutes, until very smooth. Return to pot. Slowly add up to 3 cups of reserved broth, stirring, to make a smooth, thick, and creamy consistency. Season to taste with kosher salt and freshly ground black pepper. Cook for several minutes over medium-high heat, stirring frequently.

Blanch reserved chard stems in a small amount of boiling salted water until tender, about 5 minutes. Cut into fine julienne or fine dice and scatter over each serving of soup. Serve hot.
Serves 6 (makes about 6½ cups)

roasted tomato–pepper gazpacho, basil oil

The culinary secret to this dish's intense flavor lies in the very slow roasting of red tomatoes and yellow peppers. During this process, flavors intensify and the vegetables' firm textures yield to suppleness. Caramelized juices add an extra layer of flavor. A flourish of diced tomato and peppers add the color and crunch expected in gazpacho.

6 large ripe **tomatoes**, about 2 pounds

3 large yellow **peppers**, about 1½ pounds

2 tablespoons plus 2 teaspoons **basil oil**

Preheat oven to 300°F.

Wash 5 tomatoes and remove cores. Cut in half through the stem end. Place in a large bowl. Wash 2 peppers and cut in half lengthwise. Remove stems and all the seeds. Place in bowl.

Pour 1 tablespoon basil oil over vegetables. Sprinkle with 1 teaspoon kosher salt and coarsely ground black pepper. Toss to coat thoroughly.

Place tomatoes and peppers cut side down on a baking sheet. Roast for 1 hour. Turn vegetables over. Roast for another hour. Turn over and bake an additional ½ hour (total cooking time is 2½ hours).

Place vegetables in bowl of a food processor. Add 1½ cups boiling water to baking sheet. Using a spatula, scrape up all the browned bits and accumulated juices. Add liquid and browned bits to food processor. Process soup until very smooth. Transfer soup to a bowl. Whisk in 1 tablespoon basil oil, and salt and freshly ground black pepper to taste.

Refrigerate until very cold. Add water if too thick, and adjust seasonings as needed.

Remove outer wall of remaining tomato and cut into fine dice. Finely dice remaining pepper. Scatter diced vegetables over each serving of soup and drizzle with remaining ½ teaspoon basil oil.

Serves 4 (makes about 4 cups)

zucchini foam with crab

Big-name chefs have taken to foaming everything these days, but this soup gets frothy all by itself. The skin of zucchini gives this soup its jadelike color; crab provides high-quality protein; dill provides clean, refreshing flavor.

3 medium-large **zucchini**, about 1½ pounds

1 small bunch fresh **dill**

8 ounces jumbo lump **crabmeat**

Wash zucchini thoroughly. Trim ends and cut zucchini into ½-inch chunks. Place in a 4-quart saucepan.

Wash dill and chop finely to yield 3 tablespoons. Add to pot with zucchini along with half the crabmeat and any accumulated juices from crab. Cover with 1½ cups cold water and 1 teaspoon kosher salt.

Bring to a boil. Lower heat and cover pot. Simmer for 20 minutes, until zucchini is very soft. Let cool for 5 minutes.

Transfer contents to a blender. Process until very smooth. This will take several minutes. Soup will thicken to a foamy texture.

Serve immediately or reheat gently, adding salt, if necessary, and freshly ground white pepper.

Serve with a small mound of remaining crabmeat in center of each serving of soup. Garnish with fresh dill sprigs. This is also delicious cold.

Serves 4 (makes 4 cups)

soup accompaniments

low calorie & low fat

parmesan crisps

1 long thin **Italian bread**, 8 ounces

3 tablespoons **extra-virgin olive oil** or garlic oil

2 ounces freshly grated **Parmigiano-Reggiano**

Preheat oven to 300°F.

Cut off ends of bread and discard. Freeze bread for 15 minutes. Using a serrated knife, cut bread into very thin slices on the bias. You will have about 36 slices. Distribute bread on 2 baking sheets. Place olive oil in a small dish and add a large pinch of salt. Using a pastry brush, lightly brush bread with oil. Sprinkle lightly and evenly with cheese.

Bake for about 15 minutes, until golden and crisp.

Makes 36 crisps

low calorie & low fat

lemon-poppy wafers

2 6-inch **pita breads**

2 tablespoons **lemon olive oil** (page 14, and see Note)

3 tablespoons **poppy seeds**

Preheat oven to 300°F.

Cut each bread into six equal triangles. Open each triangle and cut in half along the seam to make two triangles. You will have 24. Place triangles, split side up, on a baking sheet. Using a pastry brush, brush lightly with lemon olive oil. Sprinkle with poppy seeds. Sprinkle lightly with kosher salt. Bake for about 15 minutes, until golden and crisp.

Makes 24 wafers

Note: Lemon-flavored olive oils from Boyajian or Land of Canaan (Israel) are available in many supermarkets and specialty food stores, and are kosher.

Red Pepper and Eggplant "Ketchup" • Yogurt-Tahini

d Beef and Asiago • Chilled Oysters, Sake-Shallot

ges' Leek Terrine with Caviar • Fancy Mixed Greens,

d Tomato Frappé • Jumbo Shrimp on the Half-Shell,

Trio of Roasted Peppers and Radish Sprouts, Creamy

tilton Dressing • Beet "Carpaccio," Lemony Tonnato

Salad with Ricotta Salata and Dill • Endive Leaves

t Cheese "Caprese," Sun-Dried Tomatoes and Basil

rcress Oil • Arugula and Warm Cherry Tomato Salad

Poached Egg • Roasted Asparagus and Orange

Dressing • Sautéed Shrimp in Corn-Milk Sauce

first courses

The legendary chef

Anton Carême, considered the founder of *la grande cuisine*, insisted that cooking must be both healthful and decorative. For me, this signals the special importance of the first course, where eye-appeal is in inverse proportion to the size of the dish.

Today's first courses are designed to make an entrance, arousing the appetite, exciting all the senses, and providing a hint of—or perhaps a coy introduction to—the meal to come. The recipes in this chapter also reflect a light naturalness, and so are balancing acts of clean, simple tastes that sparkle with acidity or saltiness, a glimmer of sweetness, or even a striking bitter note.

Here you'll find familiar ingredients to which creative, healthful twists have been added: chilled oysters with sake-shallot mignonette; jumbo shrimp with eight-vegetable granita; fancy mixed greens with tangerine vinaigrette; smoked salmon with wasabi cream, for example. These innovative dishes welcome you to the meal and then move you on to the main course—without filling you up.

In this sense, almost any recipe from the vegetable chapter would also make an appropriate first course. Even many of the main courses, in halved portions, would work beautifully: a small bowl of bok choy topped with a few perfectly steamed shrimp, for example, or a cocotte of steamed mussels al finocchio.

Let the meal begin.

six dips for crudités and steamed vegetables

A deceptively simple idea: choose three favorite vegetables (fennel, carrots, and asparagus, for example) and create a cold hors d'oeuvres plate, cutting each veggie into julienned strips, slices, coins, or other interesting shapes. Then serve each variety raw and steamed. You'll discover how shape and texture can affect taste. Serve with one or more of the following oil-free and mayonnaise-free dips, brought to you in a rainbow of colors.

beetroot-yogurt

low calorie & low fat

3 medium-large **beets** (no stems), about 1 pound

1 small clove **garlic**, peeled

½ cup plain low-fat **yogurt**

Preheat oven to 400°F.

Using a vegetable peeler or sharp knife, peel beets. Salt lightly. Wrap beets in loose pouch of foil and tightly seal at the top. Place in a pie tin or on a baking sheet. Roast for 1 ½ hours. Remove from oven. Let cool 15 minutes.

Cut beets into large chunks. Place in bowl of a food processor and process until coarsely pureed. Crush garlic and add; process briefly. Add yogurt and process for 5 seconds. The dip should be a little bit chunky. Season with kosher salt and freshly ground black pepper to taste. Chill.
Makes 2 cups

roquefort-basil

low calorie & low fat

2 cups low-fat **cottage cheese**

3 ounces ripe **Roquefort cheese**

1 large bunch fresh **basil**

Place cheeses in bowl of a food processor. Process until just blended.

Wash basil and dry thoroughly. Chop enough to yield ½ cup loosely packed. Add to cheese in processor and process until smooth. Season with kosher salt and freshly ground black pepper to taste. Chill.
Makes 2 cups

red pepper and eggplant "ketchup"

low calorie & fat-free

3 large red bell **peppers**, about 1½ pounds

1 large **eggplant**, about 1 pound

1½ tablespoons **honey**

Preheat broiler. Wash peppers and eggplant, and pat dry. Put them on a baking sheet and broil until charred and blistered on all sides, about 8 minutes.

Remove peppers from oven and put in a paper bag. Close tightly and let peppers steam for 10 to 15 minutes. (You can also use a bowl covered with a lid or a plate.) Meanwhile, set oven temperature to 400°F. Bake eggplant for 30 minutes, until very soft. Let cool.

Peel peppers, discarding stems and seeds, and place in a blender. Cut eggplant in half and scrape out flesh. Discard skin and add flesh to blender. Puree until very smooth.

Put mixture in small heavy pot. Heat over medium heat until mixture thickens, about 5 minutes. Add honey, ½ teaspoon kosher salt, and freshly ground black pepper to taste. Cook for 2 minutes. Let cool to room temperature.

Makes 1¾ cups

yogurt-tahini

low calorie & low fat

1 cup plain nonfat **yogurt**

2 tablespoons **tahini** (sesame seed paste; see Note)

½ small clove **garlic**, peeled

Put yogurt in a small bowl. Using a wire whisk, whisk in tahini until thoroughly blended. Push garlic through a garlic press to yield about ¼ teaspoon garlic pulp. Add a pinch of salt and stir in garlic pulp. Chill.

Makes 1 cup

Note: Tahini can be found in health food stores, Middle Eastern groceries, and specialty food shops. Many need to be stirred before using.

goat cheese-cilantro

5 ounces fresh **goat cheese**

1 large **shallot** (or 2 small)

1 small bunch **cilantro**

Place cheese in a food processor. Peel shallot and mince to yield 1 tablespoon. Add to processor. Wash cilantro and dry thoroughly. Add ¼ cup packed leaves to processor. Process, gradually adding 5 tablespoons cold water. Add kosher salt and freshly ground white pepper to taste. Chill.

Makes 1 cup

cucumber-scallion

¾ cup low-fat **sour cream**

½ medium **cucumber**

1 **scallion**

Put sour cream in a small bowl. Peel cucumber. Grate on large holes of a box grater. Add cucumber and its juices to bowl. Finely chop white and pale green parts of scallion, and add to bowl. Stir to incorporate. Add kosher salt and freshly ground black pepper to taste. Chill.

Makes 1 cup

honeydew "carpaccio"
with air-dried beef and asiago

low calorie & low fat

Air-dried beef, or bresaola, from northern Italy, is so flavorful that just a bit is sufficient to accent paper-thin ribbons of honeydew and shards of Asiago cheese. This is a sensory exercise in flavor and aroma, and a wonderful example of "less-is-more" ingredient harmony.

8 ounces **bresaola**, sliced paper thin

½ large ripe **honeydew melon**

Wedge of **Asiago cheese** (you will only use 1 ounce)

Using a sharp knife, cut the honeydew in half through the stem ends and remove the skin and seeds. Place flat side down on a cutting board. Using a sharp, wide vegetable peeler, slice long, paper-thin ribbons of melon. You will need 2 ounces, or 8 slices, per serving.

Cover surface of 4 large plates with melon ribbons, edges touching or slightly overlapping, leaving a 1-inch border around edge of plate.

Place air-dried beef on top of melon ribbons.

Using a wide vegetable peeler or cheese slicer, slice long shards of cheese and scatter one-quarter over each portion of beef. Pass the peppermill at the table.

Serves 4

chilled oysters, sake-shallot mignonette

Simple it may be, but a raw oyster is a fairly primal food experience; I've tamed it with a subtle dressing made of sake. Distilled from rice, sake is a bit more alcoholic than white wine, and more nuanced. In this unusual mignonette, it replaces the more traditional (and sharper) vinegar. Shallots, finely chopped and submerged in sake, are a thrilling foil for briny oysters. Another thrill: Serve with chopsticks that have been soaked in ice-cold water.

¾ cup good-quality **sake**

3 large **shallots**

32 large **oysters**, freshly shucked, on the half shell, chilled

Put sake in a small bowl. Add 6 tablespoons cold water and a large pinch of sea salt.

Put 1 tablespoon whole black peppercorns in a small plastic bag. Place on a cutting board and crush with the back of a large knife. Chop coarsely. Add to sake mixture.

Peel shallots and cut into very fine julienne strips. Add 4 tablespoons to sake mixture. Let sit for up to 1 hour.

Serve oysters on 4 large plates, on a bed of crushed ice or blanched seaweed. Serve each with a ramekin of sake mignonette.

Serves 4

smoked salmon with wasabi cream

Wasabi powder, an indispensable ingredient in my twenty-first-century pantry, is the dried root of a perennial herb often referred to as Japanese horseradish, although it is related in flavor only. It provides unique pungency and a pale green color. Mixed with lightly whipped cream, wasabi makes a cool impression atop a coral bed of smoked salmon.

1½ teaspoons **wasabi powder**

¼ cup **heavy cream**

10 ounces thinly sliced **smoked salmon**

Combine wasabi powder with 1½ teaspoons cold water to make a paste. Place heavy cream in bowl of an electric mixer. Add wasabi paste and a large pinch of salt. Beat until cream is stiff. Transfer to a small bowl. Place in freezer for 30 minutes.

Completely cover the surface of 4 large plates with slices of smoked salmon, about 2½ ounces per serving. Trim edges with a sharp knife to form a perfect circle.

Top each portion with a dollop of wasabi cream.

Serves 4

jean-georges' leek terrine with caviar

low fat

Jean-Georges Vongerichten, a four-star master of simplicity, has skillfully fashioned this sophisticated terrine from only one ingredient: the leek, a member of the onion family distinguished by its sweet, mild flavor and classic long lines. I've added low-calorie seductions: nonfat sour cream and caviar, good for the (emotional) heart.

5 pounds thin **leeks** (4 or 5 bunches)

1 cup **nonfat sour cream**

½ cup **salmon caviar**

Bring a very large pot of salted water to a boil. Cut off enough of green part of leeks to make the leeks 9 inches long. Split leeks lengthwise almost to the root, about one inch from end, leaving root ends intact. Wash thoroughly, especially between leaves. Using string, tie leeks into 4 bundles.

Put leeks in boiling water and cook over high heat for 20 minutes, until tender. Reserving ¼ cup leek-poaching liquid, drain leeks carefully and let cool.

Line a 9-by-5-by-3-inch glass loaf pan with plastic wrap so that wrap overhangs the edges of the pan.

Trim roots from leeks. Place leeks in pan, one layer with whites facing one way; then one layer the opposite way. Repeat, alternating directions until all the leeks are used. Fold plastic over leeks to tightly enclose, pressing down hard with a spatula. Cut small openings in the corners of plastic to allow liquid to flow out. Cut a heavy piece of cardboard to fit directly over leeks. Place 3 ramekins or custard cups in a row in a shallow pan and carefully invert mold so that cardboard rests directly on cups. Refrigerate for at least 24 hours.

In a small bowl, mix 1 cup sour cream with ¼ cup reserved leek-poaching liquid. Add a pinch of kosher salt, if needed, and a pinch of white pepper. Chill.

Remove leek terrine from refrigerator. Discard liquid that has accumulated in pan. Place mold on a cutting board and lift off pan. Leave the plastic on and cut carefully into 1-inch-thick slices, using a serrated knife. Remove plastic. Place slices flat on each of 8 large plates. Spoon 2 tablespoons sauce over terrine and dollop with 1 tablespoon caviar. Serve immediately.

Serves 8

fancy mixed greens, tangerine vinaigrette

low calorie

Choose your favorite mesclun mix, preferably organically grown, from a farmer's market. Tangerine juice provides vibrant flavor, and has more beta-carotene than other citrus fruits, but you may substitute blood oranges or another favorite, each in its season.

6 ounces mixed **salad greens**, about 6 cups

5 large **tangerines or oranges**

3 tablespoons **extra-virgin olive oil**

Wash greens and dry thoroughly. Place in a large bowl.

Grate rind of 1 or 2 tangerines to yield 1 teaspoon zest. Set zest aside. Cut 1 or 2 tangerines in half and squeeze 6 tablespoons juice. Place juice in a small bowl and whisk in olive oil. Add zest, sea salt, and freshly ground black pepper to taste.

Peel rind from remaining tangerines and using a small sharp knife, remove all the white pith. Carefully break tangerines apart to separate segments. (If using oranges, cut along membranes to release segments.)

Add segments to bowl with greens. Toss gently with dressing, and adjust seasonings as needed. Serve on large chilled plates.

Serves 4

plum tomato salad with bocconcini and tomato frappé

low calorie

The most popular three ingredients ever to join forces in a dish—tomatoes, basil, and mozzarella—are both salad and fat-free dressing in one.

12 large ripe **plum tomatoes**, about 1¾ pounds

12 cherry-size **mozzarella** balls (see Note)

1 large bunch **basil**

Wash tomatoes and dry thoroughly.

Cut 4 tomatoes into small pieces and place in a blender with 10 small basil leaves, 1 tablespoon water, and a large pinch of kosher salt. Process until very smooth.

Very thinly slice remaining tomatoes lengthwise. Arrange in a circular pattern on 4 large plates, making 2 overlapping concentric circles. Sprinkle with kosher salt and coarsely ground white pepper.

Place 3 small mozzarella balls in center. Tuck more basil leaves around and on top of salad. Spoon sauce around edge of salad or serve in a separate ramekin. Serve immediately.

Serves 4

Note: Polly-o makes cherry-size mozzarella balls called *ciliegine,* about ⅓ ounce each. Or you may use a 1-ounce ball or slice of fresh mozzarella for each serving.

jumbo shrimp on the half shell, "8-vegetable" granita

Eddie Schoenfeld, our friend and neighbor, is a famous foodie whose flavor palate faces East. He cooks well and simply and has taught me perhaps his *only* low-calorie dish—a remarkably flavorful way to cook shrimp. His secrets: salt the cooking water until it tastes like the ocean, and dump the cooked shrimp, still in their shells, into a big bowl of iced salt water. V-8 vegetable juice, turned into a slushy granita, makes a flavor-layored cocktail sauce.

1 cup **V-8 juice**

2 large **limes**

12 very large, uncooked **shrimp** in their shells, about 1 pound

Put V-8 juice in a small nonreactive saucepan. Cook over medium heat for about 10 minutes, until reduced to ½ cup. Let cool. Grate rind of 1 lime to yield ½ teaspoon zest. Cut lime in half and squeeze 1 tablespoon juice. Add lime juice and zest to reduced juice with a pinch of kosher salt and freshly ground black pepper. Stir and transfer to a small dish. Put in freezer and stir every 30 minutes until a firm slushy texture forms, about 2 to 2½ hours.

Wash shrimp in cold water with several tablespoons of kosher salt. Drain. Bring a large pot of water to a rapid boil. Add lots of kosher salt—about ½ cup—so that it tastes like the ocean. Add shrimp, lower heat to medium, and cook for 3 to 4 minutes, until shrimp are just firm. Place in a bowl of ice-cold, heavily salted water to cool.

Place shrimp flat on a cutting board. Place your hand firmly on each shrimp to anchor, and using a very sharp thin-bladed knife, cut shrimp in half through the back. You will have two mirror-image pieces. Place 6 halves in a circle on each of 4 large plates. Slice remaining lime into 4 ¼-inch-thick slices. Place a lime wheel in center of each circle and place a small scoop of granita on the lime. Serve with additional thinly sliced lime.
Serves 4

wasabi clams with pickled ginger

Wasabi, referred to as Japanese horseradish, adds a resounding punch to briny clams, which are rich in iron and potassium. Translucent ginger, pickled pink, brings sweetness and verve to this flavor chord. Instead of wasabi powder, you may substitute a dab of wasabi paste, available in tubes at Asian markets and specialty stores.

24 littleneck or small cherrystone **clams**, chilled

4 tablespoons **wasabi powder**

⅓ cup pickled **ginger**, with ginger juice

If necessary, have your fishmonger pry open the clams for you but do not open completely. Store flat in a container so that you do not lose any of the clam juices.

In a small bowl, combine wasabi powder and 2 tablespoons cold water to form a thick paste.

Remove top shell of each clam and discard. With small knife, cut clam from bottom shell so it can be eaten easily.

Top each clam with a thin slice of pickled ginger. Place a small dollop of wasabi paste on each. Drizzle with a little pickled ginger juice.

To serve, place 6 clams per serving on any of the following: a mound of coarse sea salt, steamed and chilled seaweed, lemon leaves, or shaved or finely crushed ice. Serve immediately.
Serves 4

a trio of roasted peppers
and radish sprouts, creamy feta dressing

Bell peppers are native to the Americas and have been used as a food and medicine for thousands of years. Recently, I've been seeing bell peppers in most colors of the rainbow (red-orange-yellow-green-violet) and you may use any of them here. They are a terrific source of vitamin C. Feta cheese makes an exuberant dressing. The crowning touch? A tuft of New Age sprouts—you can use any kind, from daikon radish to broccoli, alfalfa to soybean.

3 each of red, yellow, and green **bell peppers**

4 ounces **feta cheese**

2 ounces organic radish sprouts, or other variety of **sprouts**

Preheat broiler. Wash peppers and pat dry.

Put peppers on a baking sheet and broil for several minutes on each side until skins are very black and blistered. Immediately seal peppers in a paper bag to steam for 10 minutes. (You can also use a bowl covered with a lid or a plate.)

Remove peppers and carefully peel or scrape away all charred skin. Cut peppers in half, and remove core and all seeds. Let cool.

Crumble cheese into bowl of a food processor. Add freshly ground black pepper to taste. Process, gradually adding 7 to 8 tablespoons cold water, until very smooth.

Arrange peppers in blocks of color on each of 4 large plates. Place a mound of sprouts in center. Drizzle with dressing and serve immediately.
Serves 6

"lamb's-quarters" lettuce and pear salad, stilton dressing

I am lucky to live fifty yards from a farmers' market that caravans to our neighborhood twice a week. The best day is Saturday when I look for seasonal ingredients in their prime while my husband looks for cute dogs to pet. Lamb's-quarters, new in my life, are a common wild green related to spinach. It is one of the most nutritious of plant foods, rich in beta-carotene and antioxidant vitamins, and can be part of yummy salads when the leaves are tender and small.

4 ounces **Stilton cheese**

2 very ripe **pears**

2 large bunches **lamb's-quarters** or baby spinach

Cut rind from Stilton. Cut Stilton into pieces and place in bowl of a food processor. Peel 1 pear and cut lengthwise into quarters. Remove seeds. Cut 3 pear quarters in half (reserve last quarter) and place in food processor with cheese. Process, gradually adding 6 tablespoons water to make a smooth, thick dressing. Add kosher salt and freshly ground black pepper to taste.

Peel remaining pear and cut into thin wedges. Cut reserved quarter into thin wedges.

Wash greens and dry thoroughly. Arrange in center of 4 large chilled plates. Tuck pear wedges in and around greens.

Spoon dressing over and around salad. Pass the peppermill at the table.

Serves 4

beet "carpaccio," lemony tonnato sauce

Ultra-thin slices of large cooked beets mimic the look of authentic carpaccio, which is usually made of thin slices of raw beef and was invented at Harry's Bar in Venice. Another riff: Instead of the usual mustard-mayo drizzle, I've substituted another northern Italian classic, a creamy, lemony tonnato (tuna) puree. Garnish with a few vitamin-rich beet greens.

12 ounces white **tuna** in vegetable oil

3 large **lemons**

3 very large **beets**, 10 to 12 ounces each, with some leaves attached

Drain tuna, reserving liquid. Place tuna and 2½ tablespoons liquid in bowl of a food processor. Grate rind of 1 or 2 lemons to yield 1 teaspoon zest. Cut lemons in half and squeeze 5 tablespoons lemon juice. Add zest, lemon juice, and ¼ cup water to food processor. Process for several minutes until very smooth. Add a pinch of kosher salt and freshly ground pepper to taste. Process again until the sauce is completely smooth, white, and creamy in texture. Chill until ready to use. (If chilling for more than 1 or 2 hours you may need to thin sauce with a little water, then process again briefly.)

Using a vegetable peeler or a sharp knife, peel beets. Cook in a large pot of boiling salted water for about 25 minutes, until just tender. Do not overcook. Transfer beets to a large bowl of cold water. Let rest until cold.

Using a long, thin-bladed knife, cut beets into very thin rounds. Arrange in slightly overlapping pattern on 7 or 8 large plates. Spoon sauce over top. Garnish with a small beet green leaf or thin slice of lemon.

Serves 7 or 8

eggplant and roasted pepper terrine

This is a showy first course for company. It requires some patience, but yields great rewards. When combined with cholesterol-reducing olive oil, peppers and eggplant produce a culinary and cardiovascular treat. The result is a multilayered vegetable napoleon bathed in rich natural juices. To make the presentation even more special, scatter finely minced peppers around the edge of the terrine slices.

2 long large **eggplants**, about 2½ pounds

6 very large **red bell peppers**, about 2½ pounds

6 tablespoons **extra-virgin olive oil**

Preheat oven to 375°F.

Peel the eggplants and cut in half crosswise. Cut each half, lengthwise, into long slices about ⅛-inch thick. Sprinkle lightly with kosher salt and place in a colander. Place a pot full of water on top to weight down. Let drain in sink for 30 minutes.

Meanwhile, wash peppers and cut them in half lengthwise. Remove core and seeds, then place peppers cut side down in a large shallow roasting pan. Drizzle with 3 tablespoons olive oil. Sprinkle with kosher salt and freshly ground black pepper. Roast for 50 minutes, until sides are blistered and peppers are soft. Peel skins from peppers and discard. Reserve all juices from pan. Set aside.

Wash salt off eggplant slices and pat dry. In several batches, cook eggplant in the remaining oil in a large nonstick skillet. Add ½ teaspoon oil at a time and cook eggplant 2 minutes on each side.

Add more oil to the pan and repeat until you've cooked all the eggplant.

Place reserved pepper juices in bottom of 9-by-5-by-3-inch glass loaf pan. Beginning with eggplant, make a layer to cover bottom, in slightly overlapping slices. Add an even layer of peppers, and repeat alternating layers until you've used up all the eggplant and peppers, ending with a layer of eggplant.

Lower oven temperature to 350°F. Bake terrine for 30 minutes. Press down firmly with spatula and bake 15 minutes longer. Remove from oven. Let cool. Cover terrine with plastic wrap and weight down (use a loaf pan of similar size filled with cans). Refrigerate for 24 to 48 hours. Unmold and cut into 8 slices.

Serve with any accumulated juices.

Serves 8

1-2-3 tomato salad with ricotta salata and dill

Sporting the colors of a traffic signal, this salad demands tomatoes at their seasonal best, from early August to the last gasp of summer. Sweet yellow tomatoes, inherently low in acid, make a beautiful sauce flecked with dill. Ricotta salata is a firm cheese made from ricotta curds that are pressed to squeeze out much of their liquid. Paper-thin slices of feta cheese can be substituted.

8 large ripe **tomatoes**: 3 red, 3 yellow, 2 green

1 bunch fresh **dill**

3 ounces **ricotta salata**

Wash tomatoes and remove cores. Reserve 1 yellow tomato.

Slice tomatoes into ⅙-inch-thick rounds and arrange in overlapping concentric circles on 4 large plates. Begin with an outer circle of red, then yellow, then green in center.

Sprinkle lightly with sea salt and freshly ground black pepper.

Cut reserved yellow tomato in half and place in a blender. Add a pinch of sea salt, 2 tablespoons finely chopped dill, and 2 tablespoons water. Process until very smooth.

Cut cheese into very thin slices. Place over tomatoes. Drizzle with dressing and garnish with additional sprigs of dill.

Serves 4

endive leaves and "endive marmalade," white balsamic vinaigrette

Torpedoes of the once-exotic Belgian endive are here served both raw and cooked, slowly braised into an intensely flavored vegetable jam. This simple salad achieves complexity by hitting all the flavor notes: sour, salty, bitter, and sweet, provided in large part by white balsamic vinegar, which is both acidic and sweet. Slender raw endive leaves form the petals of a flower with a spoonful of "marmalade" as its center.

7 large Belgian **endives**

3 tablespoons **extra-virgin olive oil**

⅔ cup **white balsamic vinegar** (see Note)

Trim bottoms from 3 endives. Remove any dark spots on outer leaves. Cut endives into ¼-inch slices on the bias. In a large nonstick skillet, heat 1 tablespoon olive oil. Add endive slices and cook over high heat for 5 minutes. Lower heat to medium and cook for 20 minutes. During cooking, gradually add 4 tablespoons vinegar, and season to taste with kosher salt and freshly ground black pepper. Stir frequently: You want the endives to caramelize slowly (they will look like brown sautéed onions) and to absorb all the vinegar. If the endives brown too quickly, add 1 to 2 tablespoons water. When soft and dark brown, remove from heat. Let cool.

In a small bowl, whisk together 2 tablespoons oil, 2½ tablespoons vinegar, and kosher salt and pepper to taste. Place remaining vinegar in small saucepan over medium heat and cook until syrupy and reduced by half. Let cool.

When ready to serve, trim bottoms from remaining endives. Remove outer leaves and arrange in a flower pattern (using leaves as "petals") on 4 plates. Slice interior portion on the bias and place in center of "flower."

Top the center with a portion of endive "marmalade." Drizzle with vinaigrette and a bit of reduced balsamic vinegar. Serve immediately. *Serves 4*

Note: White balsamic vinegar is available in many supermarkets.

yogurt cheese "caprese," sun-dried tomatoes and basil

The process of draining the liquid from yogurt yields a semisolid "cheese" with tangy flavor and an ultra-creamy texture. Use instead of mozzarella for a New Age "insalata caprese."

3 cups plain nonfat **yogurt**

4 ounces **sun-dried tomatoes** in oil, about ½ cup

1 bunch fresh **basil**

Line a 3-cup ceramic heart-shaped "coeur à la crème" mold with enough cheesecloth to overhang sides of mold. (Alternately, you may use a small coarse-mesh sieve, or a disposable aluminum-coated pan poked with holes.) Fill with yogurt, leveling the top with a knife. Fold flaps of cheesecloth over the top. Place on a rack in a shallow pan to catch liquid. Refrigerate for 12 to 18 hours.

Carefully turn mold upside down on a platter. Remove cheesecloth. Sprinkle top with fine sea salt and freshly ground black pepper.

Top with pieces of sun-dried tomato and drizzle with oil. Tuck leaves of fresh basil under and around tomatoes. Serve immediately.
Serves 6

poached salmon, cilantro-yogurt sauce

The best way I know to poach salmon quickly and keep all the delicious juices intact is to wrap the fillets in plastic wrap and gently lower into a shallow bath of simmering water (see Equipment, page 15). Briefly cooked, the fish remains remarkably moist. A simple sauce of yogurt and fresh cilantro adds calcium, protein, and complementary flavor notes.

1 cup plain nonfat **yogurt**

1 bunch **cilantro**, enough to make ⅓ cup packed leaves with extra sprigs for garnish

2 thick **salmon steaks**, about 8 ounces each

Place yogurt in bowl of a food processor. Wash cilantro and dry thoroughly. Pick off enough leaves to make ⅓ packed cup and add to processor. Add pinch of salt, freshly ground black pepper, and 2 tablespoons water. Process until smooth, thick, and creamy. Refrigerate until ready to use.

Cut each salmon steak into 2 long, symmetrical pieces, cutting away from the small, round center bone. Discard bone. Season lightly with salt and freshly ground white pepper. Wrap each piece in one layer of plastic wrap.

In a 12-inch skillet, bring 1½ inches of water to a boil. Add fish and cook over medium-high heat for 30 seconds. Carefully turn fish over and cook for 30 seconds longer. Cover skillet and turn off heat. Let sit for 10 minutes. Remove fish with spatula and place on a flat dish. Let cool. Refrigerate until cold.

When ready to serve, spoon a puddle of sauce in centers of 4 large plates. Remove wrap, skin, and any small bones from fish. Place on sauce. Garnish with a few sprigs of cilantro.
Serves 4

julienned beefsteak tomato salad, watercress oil

Ancient Greeks and Romans believed that watercress cured madness. Early settlers brought watercress to America for its antiscurvy properties. The settlers were right: This peppery plant contains useful amounts of vitamin C. I expect you'll be mad for this salad, whose nutritional attributes are enhanced with tomatoes and good olive oil.

2 large bunches **watercress,** about ½ pound

3 large ripe **beefsteak tomatoes**, about 10 ounces each

3 tablespoons **extra-virgin olive oil**

Wash watercress and dry thoroughly. Pluck thick stems from 1 bunch and discard (reserve the other bunch and set aside for later). Bring a small pot of salted water to a boil. Add plucked watercress and blanch for 1 minute. Drain immediately in a colander under cold water. Squeeze out excess water.

Place cooked watercress in bowl of a food processor. Add 2½ tablespoons olive oil and 2 tablespoons water. Process until smooth. Add sea salt and freshly ground black pepper to taste.

Process again and set aside.

Wash tomatoes. Cut into ¼-inch-thick slices vertically. Cut each slice into julienned strips, about ¼-inch thick. Toss with remaining ½ tablespoon oil, and sea salt and pepper.

Arrange julienned tomatoes in center of 4 large plates. Divide remaining watercress into 4 bunches, removing most of the thick stems. Place watercress on and around tomatoes. Drizzle with watercress oil.

Serves 4

arugula and warm cherry tomato salad

low calorie

This hot-and-cold salad delivers wonderful contrasts of temperature and flavor: Yellow and red cherry tomatoes release their sweet juices into a pool of garlicky oil and make a colorful warm compote atop slightly bitter greens. Nutritional virtues include antioxidant vitamins C and E and beta-carotene.

2 large bunches **arugula**

1 pint each of very small red and small yellow **cherry tomatoes** (about 24 each)

2 tablespoons plus 2 teaspoons **garlic olive oil** (page 14)

Wash arugula well, removing thick stems. Dry thoroughly. Divide arugula among 4 large plates.

Wash cherry tomatoes and cut in half through the stem end.

Heat garlic olive oil in a large nonstick skillet. Add halved tomatoes and cook over high heat for 5 minutes, until tomatoes soften and release some of their juices. (Do not overcook, as you want the tomatoes to hold their shape.)

Season with sea salt and freshly ground black pepper. Spoon warm tomatoes and pan juices evenly over arugula. Serve immediately.

Serves 4

seared smoked salmon, cucumbers pressé

low calorie

It's unusual to cook smoked salmon, but the results are intriguing—the salmon becomes a warm and silky exaggeration of itself. Here the salmon sits atop a contrastingly cool pile of wafer-thin cucumbers whose flavor is equally concentrated because they've been salted and weighted to extract their liquid.

2 large firm **cucumbers**, about 1½ pounds

2 tablespoons **lemon olive oil** (page 14, and see Note)

1 pound best-quality **smoked salmon** with skin, cut in one piece from center of fish

Wash cucumbers and, using a vegetable peeler, peel the skin in thin alternating strips to create stripes. Slice cucumbers into paper-thin rounds. Place in a colander and toss with 1 tablespoon kosher salt. Weight down and place in a shallow casserole or in the sink. Let sit 1 hour.

Wash off salt under running water. Press cucumbers between your hands to extract as much water as posslble. Transfer to a bowl. Add 1 tablespoon lemon oil, a pinch of kosher salt if needed, and freshly ground black pepper to taste. Chill until ready to serve.

Cut salmon into 6 thick strips across the width of the fish. Heat a large nonstick skillet until very hot (almost to smoking point). Coat skillet with ½ tablespoon lemon oil. Add fish, skin side down, and cook for 2 to 3 minutes, until skin is crisp. Continue to cook on all sides, 1 minute each, or until outside turns golden. Do not overcook, as the interior should be rare.

Place cucumbers in centers of 6 large plates and top with hot salmon. Drizzle with remaining lemon olive oil. Serve immediately.

Serves 6

Note: Lemon-flavored olive oils from Boyajian or Land of Canaan (Israel) are available in many supermarkets and specialty food stores, and are kosher. Be sure not to use the pure lemon oil generally used in baking.

parmesan-crusted asparagus, poached egg

A Milanese specialty, this rustic trio of ingredients seems too rich to be good for you, and yet it is. Asparagus is a good source of vitamin E, some of the B vitamins, and beta-carotene (a precursor to vitamin A). Cheese and eggs add calcium and protein.

1¾ pounds medium **asparagus**

1¾ ounces freshly grated **Parmigiano-Reggiano**

4 medium **eggs**

Preheat broiler.

Snap off woody bottoms (about an inch) from asparagus. Trim bottom of spears with a sharp knife to make even.

With a vegetable peeler, peel asparagus, using a light touch. Discard peelings. Bring a medium pot of salted water to a boil. Add asparagus and cook, uncovered, over medium heat for 6 to 7 minutes, or until just tender and bright green. Drain and refresh under cold water. Pat dry.

Divide asparagus among 4 large ovenproof plates, or 1 large platter, placing spears in one layer, side by side.

Reserving 4 teaspoons cheese, sprinkle each portion of asparagus with 2 tablespoons cheese, or sprinkle asparagus on the platter with all the remaining cheese. Place under broiler until cheese turns golden brown and begins to crisp. Remove from oven. Let cool.

Meanwhile, in a large nonstick skillet, bring 1 inch of salted water to a simmer. Crack eggs and gently slip them into water. Cook until yolks begin to set, but are still runny.

Using a slotted spoon, remove eggs from water, draining well. Blot gently on a paper towel.

Place an egg in the center of each plate on asparagus, or arrange evenly on top of asparagus on the platter. Sprinkle eggs with coarse salt, reserved cheese (about 1 teaspoon per egg), and coarsely cracked black pepper. Serve immediately.

Serves 4

roasted asparagus and orange salad, asparagus "fettuccine"

This is a dazzling and deceptive dish because you use the skin of asparagus to make starch-free "fettuccine" that fool the palate because they don't taste the way your eyes say they should. The dressing is a heart-healthy cocktail of fresh orange juice and extra-virgin olive oil.

1¾ pounds thick **asparagus**

4 large juice **oranges**

2 tablespoons **olive oil**

Preheat oven to 500°F.

Snap off woody bottoms of asparagus and discard. Using a vegetable peeler, gently peel skin of asparagus in long thin strips. Set aside. Cut peeled asparagus spears into 3 pieces on the bias. Place cut asparagus in a bowl with ½ tablespoon olive oil, ½ teaspoon kosher salt, and freshly ground black pepper. Toss to coat thoroughly.

Transfer asparagus to a baking sheet, making one layer. Roast for 12 minutes, shaking several times to prevent sticking.

Meanwhile, grate rind of 1 orange to yield ½ teaspoon zest. Cut 2 oranges in half and squeeze ½ cup juice. Place juice, 1½ tablespoons oil, and zest in a blender. Blend until slightly emulsified. Add a pinch of sea salt and pepper to taste. Set aside.

Peel and segment remaining oranges: Using a small sharp knife, cut off the 2 polar ends of each orange. Cut down the sides of the oranges to remove all peel and white pith. Gently cut along the side of each segment, right next to the membrane, and out again at the next membrane, releasing segment but leaving membrane behind. Set aside.

Transfer asparagus with any oil back to bowl. Cover to keep warm.

Bring a medium pot of salted water to a boil. Add reserved asparagus peelings ("fettuccine") and cook for 5 to 6 minutes until bright green and tender. Drain in a colander and refresh under cold water. Pat dry.

Carefully toss asparagus with orange segments. Add salt and pepper to taste. Mound in centers of 4 large plates. Top with asparagus "fettuccine." Pour dressing over salad. Serve slightly warm or at room temperature.

Serves 4

wilted fennel and grape tomato salad, tomato dressing

"Grape" tomatoes are nature's candy. Fennel tastes like licorice. Sautéed together they make a sensual and savory starter. Folklore says fennel is one of the best plants for upset digestive systems. (Hippocrates recommended it for stimulating milk production in nursing mothers.) Pulpy and thick-skinned, grape tomatoes make a flavorful and creamy dressing when pureed.

1 pint **grape tomatoes**

3 tablespoons **extra-virgin olive oil**

1 large **fennel** bulb, about 1½ pounds, with fronds

Wash tomatoes. Cut 12 tomatoes in half. Place in a blender with 1 tablespoon oil and 1 tablespoon water. Process until very smooth. Add kosher salt and freshly ground black pepper to taste. Set sauce aside, but do not refrigerate.

Wash fennel, removing any brown spots. Trim bottom. Remove feathery fronds from fennel stalks. Set fronds aside. Slice stalks into paper-thin rounds, about 2 cups, and reserve. Slice bulb into paper-thin slices through the root end.

Heat 2 tablespoons oil in a large nonstick skillet.

Add fennel slices and sauté over high heat for 5 minutes, stirring constantly. Add remaining grape tomatoes and cook for 1 to 2 minutes longer, just until tomatoes soften. Add sea salt and pepper to taste. Remove from heat. Let cool to room temperature.

Mound fennel and tomatoes in centers of 4 large plates. Finely chop reserved fennel fronds and sprinkle over salad. Spoon sauce around and on top of salad. Serve immediately.

Serves 4

sautéed shrimp in corn-milk sauce

Corn was first grown in central Mexico more than seven thousand years ago, when all parts of the plant were utilized as food or medicine. In that spirit, I use the kernels, the cob, and the husks (for garnish), in this rather striking recipe. A gluten-free grain, corn provides significant amounts of fiber, and carbohydrates for energy. It delivers an indescribable sweetness when "corn milk" is simply extracted from fresh kernels and blended with a broth made from boiled cobs. Thickened with a touch of chilled whipped butter, the sweet juices become a silky sauce for protein-rich, low-calorie shrimp.

36 medium **shrimp** in their shells, about 1 pound

2 unhusked ears **corn**

4 tablespoons unsalted whipped **butter**

Remove shells from shrimp, leaving tails on. Place shells in a 4-quart pot.

Shuck corn and discard corn silk. Reserve corn husks for garnish. Cut kernels from cobs, using a thin-bladed sharp knife, cutting as close to the cob as possible. Set kernels aside. You will have about 2 cups.

Break cobs into several pieces and add to pot. Cover shells and cobs with cold water. Add 1 teaspoon sea salt and ½ teaspoon whole black peppercorns. Bring to a boil. Cover pot and cook over medium heat for 20 minutes.

Strain broth through a fine-mesh sieve. Add 1 cup broth and 1 cup corn kernels to a blender. Add 3 tablespoons whipped butter. Puree until very smooth. Strain through a coarse-mesh sieve into a small saucepan. Add sea salt and freshly ground black pepper to taste.

In a large nonstick skillet, melt 1 tablespoon whipped butter. Add shrimp and 1 cup corn kernels. Cook over medium heat, stirring often, until shrimp turn opaque, about 3 minutes. Meanwhile, heat sauce and cook over high heat for 1 to 2 minutes.

Divide shrimp and corn mixture evenly among 6 shallow soup bowls. Spoon sauce over. Garnish with 2 long strips of corn husks.

Serves 6

Polenta Tart with Melted Tomatoes and Smoked Mozzarella • Baked Fennel
Sardinia • Orecchiette with Broccoli, Broccoli-Butter Sauce • Penne with Z
al Finocchio, Toasted Fennel Fronds • Smoky Shrimp with Steamed Bok Choy
• Lacquered Salmon, Pineapple-Soy Reduction • Bay-Steamed Halibut wi
Swordfish with Fresh Corn, Chipotle "Cream" • Pepper-Seared Mahi Mah

Vermouth • Chilean Sea Bass on Braised Savoy Cabba
under a Brick, Whole-Poached Scallions • Sautèed Coc
Bass, Parsley-Garlic Sauce • Layered Flounder and
Preserved Lemon Sauce • Miso-Glazed Grouper, Jap
Seared • Lemon-Thyme Roast Chicken with Pan Juic
Double-Strength Sherry Consommé • Cold Poached C
Chicken on the Bone • Sautéed Chicken Breasts with Oven-Dried Grapes •
Hens with Sumac and Shallots • Turkey Salad with Grape Tomatoes and
Roast with Fresh Sage and Baked Pears • Duck Magret with Roasted Red Or
with Orange-Chipotle Jus • Pork Tenderloin with Sweet Mustard and Roser
Cumin-Crusted Lamb with Apricots • Lamb Chops Provençal • Rib-Eye Roast, Gra

rmigiana • Whole-Wheat Linguine in the Style of

chini, Zucchini-Garlic Sauce • Steamed Mussels

d Oyster Sauce • Salmon Arrosto with Rosemary

Lemon Oil • Basil-Stuffed Swordfish • Seared

Mango Salsa • Baked Artic Char with Dill and

• Salmon Demi-Cuit, Sauce Moutarde • Bluefish

th Asparagus, Asparagus Veloutè • Steamed Sea

moked Salmon • Lemon Sole in Tomato and

se-Style • Next Wave Tuna Salad: Tartare and

• Chicken Velvet Salad • Chicken and Leeks in

ken, Avocado and Mango Mousseline • Tandoori

icken Chaud-Froid with Yogurt-Lime Glaze • Red

chini, Zucchini Coulis • Rolled and Tied Turkey

s and Pomegranate Molasses • Brined Pork Loin

• Potted Leeks and Corned Beef in Riesling •

Style • Boeuf à la Ficelle with Shiitakes and Ginger

main courses

This chapter contains luxurious-sounding, full-flavored entrees whose range addresses the needs of everyone and whose tastes reflect the globalization of the new American kitchen.

All the recipes are low in calories, and a third of them are low in fat. For vegans there are dishes based solely on vegetables; for "ovo-lactos" there are vegetable and pasta main courses incorporating butter, cream, and cheese (in a healthy cookbook, yes!); for the less doctrinaire there are crustacean and fish dishes, and lots of chicken and turkey choices.

Even pork, lamb, and beef fit into this healthful paradigm—not because they're the focus of trendy high-protein diets of questionable durability, but because in sensible amounts they belong in the 1-2-3 diet. After all, this is not a book about deprivation but about being able to eat *everything*. Significantly lowered calorie and fat content is not achieved by limiting quantities and excluding certain foods from your life, as most diets and health-oriented cookbooks demand. It's achieved through the skillful combination of the very best ingredients—resulting in dishes that will surprise you with their intense flavors.

Generous main course offerings engage all the senses, and deliver all the dimensions of taste: the qualities of sour, salty, bitter, sweet, and umami—a Japanese word that describes the meatlike, savory taste of foods like wild mushrooms, parmesan cheese, miso, and ripe tomatoes. It is the flavor sensation of naturally occurring monosodium glutamate. There is a synergistic effect when umami foods are added to other ingredients, unlocking and intensifying the essence of a dish—and of course you will find many of these combinations here.

The main objective: To achieve depth of flavor. Recent studies show that boosting flavors actually reduces hunger. You don't need to eat a *lot* to feel satisfied, just *well*.

Many of these recipes require slow cooking—braising, caramelizing, and roasting—to develop their flavors and richness. But great taste can also be achieved by leaving well enough alone, as in Steamed Sea Bass with Parsley-Garlic Sauce (page 82), or by manipulating one ingredient in several ways, as in Sautéed Cod with Asparagus and Asparagus Velouté (page 81).

Many of these dishes are important sources of high-quality protein, supplying all of the amino acids required by the body for good health. They also supply fat, but based on endless experimentation, many of the main courses qualify as low fat, in addition to being low in calories. Those watching their fat intake might balance their entree selection with a fat-free or low-fat vegetable or side dish.

These recipes in particular prove that simplicity should never be confused with lack of sophistication. Nowhere is this more evident than at the heart of the meal.

polenta tart with melted tomatoes and smoked mozzarella

For your favorite vegetarian, polenta is a sturdy carbohydrate made of ground corn—but it needs a flavor boost. Here it is crowned with meaty slow-roasted tomatoes and baked with smoky mozzarella into a rich vegetarian main course.

12 plum **tomatoes**

4 ounces **smoked mozzarella**

1 cup stone-ground yellow **cornmeal**

Preheat oven to 275°F.

Wash tomatoes. Cut 10 in half lengthwise. Sprinkle cut sides lightly with fine sea salt.

Line a baking sheet with parchment paper or foil and bake tomatoes, cut side down, for 1 hour. Turn over and bake for 1 hour longer. Turn again and bake for 30 minutes longer. Remove from oven.

Meanwhile, shred cheese on large holes of a box grater.

In a medium pot, bring 3½ cups water and 1 teaspoon salt to a boil. Slowly add cornmeal, whisking with a wire whisk until completely integrated, about 5 minutes. Switch to a wooden spoon. Stir in half the cheese. Continue to cook over medium heat for 5 minutes, stirring constantly, until polenta is very thick but still creamy.

Heat oven to 375°F.

Coat an 8½-inch removable-bottom tart pan with nonstick vegetable spray. Pour polenta into pan, smoothing the top. Thinly slice remaining tomatoes and place around perimeter of tart, overlapping slightly. Place cooked tomatoes, cut side down, on polenta, in a circular pattern, and sprinkle with remaining cheese. Bake for 6 to 8 minutes. Place under broiler until golden. Serve warm.

Serves 4

---

baked fennel parmigiana

A startling reduction of V-8 creates an intense, silky tomato sauce that's low in calories but packed with vitamins and minerals. It blankets thick wedges of cooked fennel, baked under a mantle of the best parmesan cheese. This is a delicious side dish, too.

1 large **fennel** bulb, about 1½ pounds

1½ cups **V-8** juice

2 ounces freshly grated **Parmigiano-Reggiano**

Cut feathery fronds from fennel and set aside. Trim fennel bulb and cut lengthwise through the core into 4 wedges.

Place wedges in a large pot. Add water to just cover. Add 1 tablespoon kosher salt and bring to a boil. Cook for 20 minutes over medium-high heat until just barely tender. Drain thoroughly.

Preheat oven to 400°F.

Put V-8 in a small saucepan and cook over medium heat until reduced to 1 cup.

Place fennel, cut side up, in a shallow ovenproof casserole. Pour ¾ cup reduced V-8 over fennel. Sprinkle with cheese and pour remaining juice over.

Bake for 30 minutes, until cheese is golden brown. Sprinkle with chopped fennel fronds. Serve hot.

Serves 2

whole-wheat linguine in the style of sardinia

This brings me back to the Costa Smerelda, where blue skies, emerald seas, and simple sardine dishes are daily realities. Whole-grain pasta adds many nutrients, and sardines are a valuable source of omega-3 fatty acids. Celery Gratinée with Prosciutto (page 114) makes a compatible side dish.

28 ounces canned **plum tomatoes** in thick puree

3¾ ounces **sardines** packed in oil, skinless and boneless

8 ounces dried **whole-wheat linguine**

Place tomatoes, sardines, and their oil in a 4-quart pot. Add ¼ teaspoon whole black peppercorns and a large pinch of kosher salt and bring to a boil. Lower heat to maintain a simmer and cover pot. Cook for 30 minutes, stirring frequently with a wooden spoon to break up sardines. Uncover pot and cook for 30 minutes longer over low heat. Mixture should be rather thick and chunky.

Bring a large pot of salted water to a boil. Add linguine and cook for 12 to 15 minutes, or until tender. Drain thoroughly in a colander and transfer to a large bowl or individual shallow soup bowls.

Heat sauce and pour over hot linguine. Serve immediately.

Serves 4

orecchiette with broccoli, broccoli-butter sauce

Orecchiette, "little ears" of pasta, provide a textural backdrop for much-lauded broccoli, which here is used in its entirety; briefly cooked florets, and boiled stems, enriched with a bit of butter to produce an original and very comforting sauce.

1 large head **broccoli**

3 tablespoons unsalted **butter,** chilled

8 ounces **orecchiette pasta**

Cut broccoli into small florets, leaving only ½ inch of small stems. Set aside.

Using a vegetable peeler, peel the thick stalks. Cut into 1-inch pieces. Place in a saucepan with 1¼ cups salted water. Bring to a boil, lower heat to medium, and cook, covered, for 25 minutes. When very soft, transfer stalks and cooking liquid to a blender. Puree until very smooth. Cut the butter into small pieces, add to puree, and process, adding a little water if necessary to make a smooth sauce. Add sea salt and freshly ground black pepper to taste and transfer to a saucepan.

Meanwhile, cook the pasta in a large pot of boiling salted water for about 10 minutes. Add broccoli florets and cook another 3 to 4 minutes, until broccoli is tender and bright green and pasta is cooked through. Drain pasta in a colander, then transfer to a large bowl, platter, or individual shallow soup bowls.

Heat the sauce gently and pour over the drained pasta and broccoli. Pass the peppermill at the table.

Serves 4

penne with zucchini, zucchini-garlic sauce

With a silky sauce fashioned from zucchini and heart-healthy olive oil, this is a simple yet luxurious pasta dish. Little cubes of zucchini add textural interest to the penne. For this dish, cook the pasta until it is just beyond al dente: This makes for larger portions, and the softer texture complements the tender zucchini cubes. Use tri-colored penne for visual appeal; use whole-wheat penne for added fiber and nutrients; and, of course, use imported Italian pasta for better flavor. Use Jerusalem artichoke pasta if you're allergic to gluten.

4 medium **zucchini**, about 1½ pounds

4 tablespoons **garlic olive oil** (page 14) or store-bought

8 ounces **penne pasta**

Wash zucchini and cut 1½ zucchini into thick rounds. Cut rounds in half and place in a small saucepan. Add enough salted water to just cover. Bring to a boil. Lower heat and cover pan. Cook for 15 minutes. Using a slotted spoon, transfer zucchini to a blender. Add ½ cup cooking water and 1 teaspoon garlic olive oil. Process until very smooth. Add kosher salt and freshly ground black pepper to taste. Set aside.

Trim ends of remaining zucchini and discard. Cut zucchini as meticulously as possible into ¼-inch cubes.

Heat remaining garlic olive oil in a large non-stick skillet, add zucchini cubes, and sauté over high heat until zucchini softens and turns golden. Add a liberal amount of salt and pepper to taste. Keep warm.

Bring a large pot of salted water to a rapid boil. Add pasta and cook for 12 to 14 minutes until pasta is tender, a bit longer than for al dente.

Drain pasta thoroughly. Divide among 4 shallow soup bowls. Distribute cooked zucchini and oil evenly over pasta. Heat zucchini-garlic sauce and pour over pasta. Add a grinding of pepper. Serve immediately.

Serves 4

steamed mussels al finocchio, toasted fennel fronds

low calorie & low fat

Chicken broth might seem unexpected in this shellfish dish, but so is the result. Virtually fat-free, this up-front flavor merger reflects a trend among modern chefs of cooking sea creatures in meat and poultry essences. Fennel is a two-in-one addition: the bulb becomes a textural vegetable component and the fronds, toasted and crumbled, become a crunchy garnish.

1¾ pounds medium-large **mussels**

1 large **fennel** bulb with lots of feathery fronds, about 1½ pounds

4 cups low-sodium **chicken stock**

Remove "beards" from mussels and scrub thoroughly under cold running water. Set aside.

Remove all feathery fronds from fennel and set aside for later. Trim fennel bulb. Thinly slice stalks of fennel and finely chop trimmed fennel bulb.

Put stock in a 6-quart pot. Add sliced and chopped fennel. Add ½ teaspoon coarsely ground black pepper. Bring to a boil. Lower heat to medium and cook for 10 minutes, until fennel is just tender.

Add mussels and increase heat to medium-high. Cover pot and cook for 10 minutes, shaking pot frequently to distribute mussels.

Meanwhile, coarsely chop fennel fronds and place in a small nonstick skillet. Add a pinch of kosher salt and cook over medium-high heat for several minutes, until fennel fronds give up their moisture and are dry. Set aside.

When the mussels have opened (discard any that haven't), transfer them with a slotted spoon to a large bowl. Cover with an inverted bowl or plate to keep warm. Increase heat to high and boil liquid for 5 minutes, until reduced to 3 cups or less. Pour through fine-mesh sieve over mussels. Toss and divide between 2 large soup bowls. Garnish with toasted fennel fronds. Serve immediately.

Serves 2

smoky shrimp with steamed bok choy and oyster sauce

low calorie & low fat

The shrimp here are "dry-seared" in their shells, which imparts a slightly smoky flavor. Bok choy, a sexy Asian cabbage with a narrow waist and green leaves for a hat, is high in calcium and potassium. The two are bound gastronomically by Chinese oyster sauce, which you'll find in your supermarket's Asian section.

16 very large **shrimp** in their shells, about 1 pound

5 or 6 small **bok choy**, or 1 large, about 1 pound

3 tablespoons **Chinese oyster sauce**

Wash shrimp, leaving shells and tails intact. Sprinkle lightly with salt. Heat a large nonstick skillet until very hot. Add shrimp and cook briefly over high heat until shells become opaque and get a bit charred. Shrimp will not be fully cooked. Remove from heat and let cool. Peel shrimp, leaving tails on.

Wash bok choy, separating stalks. Cut into ½-inch pieces, including the greens. Bring a large pot with three inches of water, fitted with a steamer basket, to a boil. Place bok choy in steamer and cover tightly. Steam for 15 minutes, until soft.

Transfer bok choy to a bowl, making sure to drain any liquid. Place shrimp in steamer and cover. Steam over boiling water for 1 minute.

Quickly toss bok choy with oyster sauce, adding lots of coarsely ground black pepper. Top with steamed shrimp. Serve immediately.

Serves 2

salmon arrosto with rosemary

Few things are better than a side of salmon roasting in a mound of rosemary. Salmon is rich in EPA and DHA, two omega-3 fatty acids, known for their beneficial effect on the heart and immune system. Pinelike rosemary, rarely used with fish, complements salmon's rich flavor, and is especially appropriate since the word *rosemary* means "dew of the sea" (*ros* = dew, *marinus* = of the sea).

2 large bunches **rosemary**

1 large **red onion**

2-pound **salmon** fillet cut from center of fish, skin on

Preheat oven to 500°F.

Wash rosemary and pat dry. Place 1 bunch on shallow baking sheet. Peel onion and thinly slice. Distribute on top of rosemary.

With tweezers, remove any bones from the salmon. Season salmon with kosher salt and freshly ground black pepper. Place on onions, skin side down. Cover fish with remaining bunch of rosemary, saving a few sprigs for garnish.

Roast for 20 minutes. Fish will be moist. Do not overcook.

Remove fish from oven. Transfer to a platter with cooked onions. Serve with sprigs of fresh rosemary.

Serves 4

lacquered salmon, pineapple-soy reduction

A reduction of pineapple juice and Japanese soy sauce (shoyu) becomes a magical glaze for strong-flavored fish. The first forkful paints your palate with sweet, salty, and acidic notes. Pineapple's potassium balances the sodium in shoyu. This is also an excellent preparation with fresh tuna.

2 cups unsweetened **pineapple juice**

4 teaspoons **Japanese shoyu** or tamari (see Note)

4 6½-ounce thick **salmon** steaks

Put pineapple juice in a small nonreactive saucepan. Bring to a boil. Lower heat to medium and cook until juice is reduced to 1 cup. Transfer to a small bowl and let cool.

Mix shoyu with reduced pineapple juice.

Place salmon in a shallow casserole. Pour pineapple-soy mixture over fish. Refrigerate and marinate for 2 hours, turning after the first hour.

Heat a large nonstick skillet or 2 smaller non-stick skillets until hot. Sear fish for 3 minutes on each side or until cooked through. Be careful not to overcook.

Meanwhile, place remaining pineapple-shoyu mixture in a small saucepan and cook over medium-low heat until reduced by half, about 5 minutes. Using a pastry brush, glaze top of salmon with a little of the reduced marinade and remove salmon from the pan. Serve each portion with some of the remaining marinade. Serve immediately.

Serves 4

Note: Traditional Japanese soy sauce, or shoyu, is made from fermented soy beans, wheat, and salt, and has a highly complex flavor. Commercial brands—made, usually, with hydrolized vegetable protein, salt, flavorings, and caramel flavor—are not good substitutes. Tamari, usually made without wheat, is a bit heavier, but quite acceptable.

bay-steamed halibut with lemon oil

Bay leaves, also known as laurel, were used as purifying herbs and as symbols of wisdom and glory. Here, glorious halibut rests on its laurels, steamed in a see-through pouch with a touch of lemon-scented olive oil. I prefer California bay leaves, for their graceful elongated shape and intense aroma.

4 8-ounce **halibut** steaks

20 whole California **bay leaves**, dried or fresh

8 teaspoons **lemon olive oil** (page 14, and see Note)

Place each piece of fish on a large square of plastic wrap (see Equipment, page 15) and season with salt and freshly ground black pepper. Place 5 bay leaves side-by-side to cover one side of each steak, and drizzle with 1 teaspoon lemon olive oil. Wrap tightly in plastic wrap. Refrigerate for 3 to 6 hours.

When ready to cook, bring a large pot of water, fitted with a steamer basket, to a boil. Place wrapped fish in basket and cover tightly. Steam over boiling water for 10 to 12 minutes, depending on thickness of fish, until cooked through.

Carefully remove fish from steamer and unwrap packets.

Serve immediately, drizzled with packet juices and remaining lemon olive oil. Sprinkle with coarse sea salt.

Serves 4

Note: Lemon-flavored olive oils from Boyajian or Land of Canaan (Israel) are available in many supermarkets and specialty food stores, and are kosher.

basil-stuffed swordfish

This unusual presentation features a channel of bright green basil cut into the fish, which then is marinated in a bath of olive oil. The basil impregnates the fish and oil with heady virtue. Herbalists say basil has phytochemicals that activate the body's protective enzymes. Slow poaching in a bit of the marinade imparts tenderness, and olive oil helps lower cholesterol.

6 8-ounce **swordfish** steaks, 1 inch thick, skin removed

2 large bunches fresh **basil**

1 cup **olive oil** for marinating (of which only 5 tablespoons will be eaten)

Using a small sharp knife, make a 3½-inch-long vertical slit down the center of each fish steak; do not cut through. Separate slightly with your fingers to make a channel.

Wash basil and dry thoroughly. Make six stacks of basil leaves. Roll each stack tightly and pack leaves neatly in channels of steaks.

Place swordfish in a shallow casserole. Pour olive oil over fish. Sprinkle lightly with kosher salt and coarsely ground black pepper. Marinate for 1 hour at room temperature.

Place fish steaks in 2 nonstick skillets. Add 1 tablespoon of the oil to each pan. Cook over low heat for 2 minutes. Cover pan and continue cooking for 5 minutes. Using a spatula, carefully turn fish over and cook, covered, for 5 to 6 minutes longer, or until fish is cooked through.

Remove fish from pan, turning over so that basil is showing. Serve with pan juices and garnish with fresh basil sprigs.
Serves 6

seared swordfish with fresh corn, chipotle "cream"

This "cream sauce" is dairy-free, made with the "milk" of fresh corn and thickened with canned chipotle peppers in adobo—which you'll find in Latino and specialty markets. The contrast of this spicy and naturally sweet corn sauce is stunning against the caramelized seared swordfish.

2 ears **corn**

2 small **chipotle peppers** in adobo

4 8-ounce **swordfish** steaks, about ¾-inch thick

Shuck corn and discard corn silk. Cut kernels from cobs, using a thin-bladed sharp knife. You will have about 2 cups.

Place 1½ cups kernels in a small saucepan with 1¾ cups water and a large pinch of kosher salt. Bring to a boil, lower heat, and cook until very soft, about 20 minutes. Place corn and cooking liquid in a blender with 1 small chipotle pepper and about 1 teaspoon of its adobo sauce. Puree until very smooth, adding 2 to 3 tablespoons water if too thick. Strain through a coarse-mesh sieve into a small bowl. Add salt to taste. You will have about 1 cup. This can be made in advance and refrigerated.

Place remaining corn in a saucepan with enough water to cover, and cook over medium heat for 15 minutes.

Meanwhile, lightly rub sea salt and a little adobo sauce onto both sides of swordfish steaks. Coat a large nonstick skillet with vegetable spray. Heat skillet over high heat and add swordfish. Cook for 5 minutes on each side, until golden and cooked through but still moist.

Reheat sauce gently. Drain corn. Pour sauce over fish and scatter hot cooked corn on top. Serve immediately, garnished with a small piece of remaining pepper.
Serves 4

pepper-seared mahi mahi, mango salsa

This hot/cold combo is great during a tropical heat wave, or when you're in the winter doldrums. Famous as Hawaiian island fare, mahi mahi (formerly called dolphinfish) is sweet and toothsome with appealingly large flakes when cooked carefully. A sprightly salsa of mango and cilantro adds mouthwatering flavor notes—and beta-carotene and vitamin C.

2 ripe medium **mangoes**

1 bunch fresh **cilantro**

4 9-ounce thick **mahi mahi** steaks

Peel the mangoes with a sharp knife. Carefully cut them in half and remove pits by slowly navigating knife along length of pit. Cut 1 mango into 1-inch chunks and place in a blender. Add a pinch of sea salt, 8 cilantro leaves, and 2 tablespoons cold water. Process until very smooth. Set sauce aside at room temperature.

As meticulously as possible, cut remaining mango into ¼-inch cubes and put in a small bowl. Coarsely chop enough cilantro to yield ⅓ cup. Add to mango. Add salt and pepper to taste. Stir, and chill for 30 minutes.

Scatter ½ teaspoon very coarsely ground black pepper onto one side of each fish steak, pressing firmly into flesh. Sprinkle lightly with salt. Heat a large nonstick skillet until very hot. Add fish, pepper side down, and cook for several minutes on each side over high heat, until fish is seared on the outside but still moist in the center. Remove from heat. Let rest for 2 minutes.

Serve atop a mound of mango salad, and spoon mango sauce around fish. Garnish with additional cilantro leaves.

Serves 4

baked arctic char with dill and vermouth

Arctic char is a staple among Eskimos, to whom coronary disease is almost unknown. It is a salmonlike fish rich in beneficial omega-3 fatty acids. Vermouth, a fortified aromatic wine flavored with herbs, has great affinity for fish—as does dill, whose name derives from a Norse word meaning "to lull," because it was once considered a mild sedative.

4 10-ounce **arctic char** fillets, skin on

1 cup dry **vermouth**

1 bunch fresh **dill**

Using tweezers, remove any bones from fish. Place fillets in one layer in a shallow casserole. Pour vermouth over fish.

Wash dill. Finely chop about ¾ cup and scatter over fish. Coarsely grind 1 teaspoon white peppercorns and sprinkle along with fine sea salt over fish. Marinate for 1 hour, refrigerated.

Preheat oven to 425°F.

Remove fish from casserole and place on a baking sheet. Bake for 12 to 13 minutes, depending on thickness of fish. Remove from oven. Serve immediately, garnished with tufts of remaining fresh dill.

Serves 4

chilean sea bass on braised savoy cabbage

In this recipe a little bacon goes a long way in flavoring gently braised savoy cabbage. Savoy, with its crinkly leaves, leads all other cabbages in its concentration of phytonutrients, like beta-sitosterol and pheuphytin-A—which is more than you'll ever want to know about a vegetable, except that cabbage was once called "the medicine of the poor." Chemistry aside, this is a delicious preparation for a mild, sweet-fleshed fish previously known as Patagonian toothfish and renamed for obvious reasons.

1 medium **savoy cabbage**, about 1¾ pounds

3 ounces slab **bacon**, nitrite-free

4 7-ounce thick **Chilean sea bass** fillets

Wash cabbage. Remove core and, using a long thin-bladed knife, finely cut into ¼-inch slices.

Cut bacon into ¼-inch cubes. Place in a 12-inch nonstick skillet with a cover. Cook over medium heat for about 3 minutes, until fat is rendered and bacon begins to crisp.

Add cabbage, ½ cup water, ½ teaspoon kosher salt, and freshly ground black pepper. Cook over medium-high heat for 10 minutes, stirring frequently. Add another ½ cup water and lower heat to medium. Cover skillet and cook, stirring often,

for about 30 minutes, or until cabbage is brown and soft. If cabbage begins to stick, add ¼ cup water.

Season fish with salt and pepper. Place on cabbage in skillet. Add ¼ cup water and cover skillet. Continue to cook for about 10 to 12 minutes, or until fish is cooked through.

When ready to serve, place a mound of cooked cabbage on each of 4 large plates. Carefully lift fish onto cabbage and drizzle with any pan juices. Serve immediately.
Serves 4

salmon demi-cuit, sauce moutarde

This recipe survived the nouvelle cuisine era when it was also called Salmon Unilateral. Either name indicates that heat is applied only to one side of the fish so that it gets progressively rare toward the top. Mustard, used for centuries as medicine, is here used to flavor and thicken a simple cream sauce.

4 7-ounce **salmon** fillets, skin removed

¾ cup **half-and-half**

2 tablespoons plus 2 teaspoons good-quality tarragon **mustard**

With tweezers, remove any bones from the salmon. Rub a little coarse sea salt onto one side of each fillet. Dust with freshly ground black pepper.

Coat with vegetable spray a 12-inch nonstick skillet with a cover. Heat pan until very hot and add fish, salted side up. Cook over medium-high heat for 5 to 6 minutes. The bottom of the fish will get crisp and the fish will cook from the bottom up. The top quarter of the fish will still be uncooked. Cover pan and cook for 2 to 3 minutes, until top

just begins to turn opaque. Do not overcook.

Meanwhile, put half-and-half and mustard in a small skillet. Add a pinch of salt and pepper. Cook over medium heat, whisking constantly with a wire whisk, about 1 minute, until sauce is just warm and has thickened.

Remove fish from pan. Spoon sauce around fish. Serve immediately.
Serves 4

bluefish under a brick, whole-poached scallions

Bluefish is a late summer gift whose virtues are its rich and oily flesh and soft, flaky texture. Cooking it under a brick guarantees a crisp skin, and teriyaki and scallions make a sweet and pungent foil. Scallions do double duty here, serving also as an unusual vegetable accompaniment.

4 7-ounce center-cut **bluefish** fillets, skin on

1 cup **teriyaki sauce**

3 bunches **scallions**

Remove bones from fish and discard. Place fish in a shallow casserole and cover with teriyaki sauce. Marinate for 15 minutes.

Meanwhile, trim roots from scallions. Trim 2 bunches of scallions so that each scallion has only 1 inch of dark green top. Place trimmed scallions in a skillet with enough salted water to just cover. Bring to a boil, then lower heat and cook until scallions are soft, about 5 minutes. Keep warm.

Remove fish from marinade. Reserve marinade. Season skinless side of fish with freshly ground black pepper. Heat 1 very large or 2 smaller nonstick skillets until very hot. Put fish skin side up in pan and place a foil-wrapped brick (or heavy saucepan) on fillets. Cook over medium-high heat for 3 minutes. Turn over and cook 3 minutes longer, weighted with bricks.

Finely dice remaining scallions to yield ½ cup. Add to reserved marinade. Remove bricks and add marinade to pan, with ¼ cup water. Heat for 1 to 2 minutes, or until fish is cooked as desired. Serve immediately with boiled scallions that have been quickly warmed in water and thoroughly drained. *Serves 4*

sautéed cod with asparagus, asparagus velouté

Once upon a time, asparagus was valued only for the tips, resulting in a reckless loss of nutrients and fiber. In this dish, I've spun the stalks into a sauce of velvet. Then the tips are piled atop flaky, low-fat cod.

2 pounds medium-thick **asparagus**, about 36

4 tablespoons unsalted **butter**

6 7-ounce thick **cod** fillets

Cut off top 2¾ inches of asparagus stalks and set aside. Cut woody bottoms from asparagus stalks and discard.

Peel stalks with a vegetable peeler and cut into 1-inch pieces. Place in a saucepan with enough salted water to cover. Bring to a boil, lower heat, and cook for about 10 minutes, or until stalks are very soft.

Using a slotted spoon, transfer cooked stalks to a blender. Add ¾ to 1 cup cooking liquid and process until smooth. Add 2 tablespoons butter and continue to process until very smooth. Add freshly ground black pepper and return to saucepan.

Bring a small pan of salted water to a boil. Add asparagus tips and cook until just tender, about 5 minutes.

Meanwhile, season fish generously with kosher salt and freshly ground black pepper. Melt remaining 2 tablespoons butter in a large nonstick skillet. Place fish, rounded side down, in skillet and cook over medium-high heat until golden. Turn over and cook for a few minutes longer until golden. Cover pan and cook until fish reaches desired doneness (fish should just begin to flake).

Spoon gently reheated sauce on each of 6 plates. Top with fish and drained asparagus tips, spooning a little sauce over the top. Serve immediately.

Serves 6

steamed sea bass, parsley-garlic sauce

low calorie

Parsley today is a token garnish, but in the Middle Ages it appeared in herbal medicines and was purported to cure a wide range of ills, especially those having to do with the liver and kidneys. Parsley reconsidered: It is the prototypical dark green vegetable, recommended for its antioxidants and iron, and for its historic use as a breath sweetener. Freezing the garlic oil is my special technique for adding body and ultra-creamy texture to this vibrant sauce for moist sea bass.

2½ tablespoons **garlic olive oil** (page 14)

3 large bunches curly **parsley**

4 8-ounce thick **sea bass** fillets, skin removed

Place garlic oil in a small ramekin and freeze for several hours.

Wash parsley thoroughly and dry well. Coarsely chop enough parsley leaves to yield 3 packed cups.

Bring a medium pot of salted water to a boil. Put chopped parsley in water and blanch for 1 minute. Drain in a colander and pat dry. Puree in a blender with frozen garlic oil, added in small pieces. You can do this easily with the tip of a knife. Add 1 or more tablespoons water. Blend until thick and creamy. Transfer to a small saucepan and season with freshly ground black pepper to taste.

Season fish with kosher salt and pepper. Bring a large pot with three inches of water, fitted with a flat bamboo or metal steamer basket, to a boil. Place fish in steamer and cover tightly. Steam for 10 to 12 minutes, depending on thickness of fish, until cooked through.

Carefully transfer fish to a platter or individual plates. Reheat sauce gently and spoon over the fish. Serve immediately, garnished with a few sprigs of parsley.

Serves 4

layered flounder and smoked salmon

low calorie & low fat

Built like a triple-decker sandwich, this is a recipe of alternating layers of flavor and health attributes. Flounder, white and almost fat-free, contrasts with pink smoked salmon, which contributes its distinctive taste and essential fatty acids. A shower of lemon zest pulls together the flavors of this mineral-rich dish.

5 large thin-skinned **lemons**

12 thin **flounder** fillets, about 3 ounces each

8 thin slices **smoked salmon**, about 1½ ounces each

Grate rind of lemons to yield 4 teaspoons zest.

Place 4 flounder fillets on a flat surface. Top each with a similar-shaped slice of smoked salmon. Sprinkle with a little grated lemon zest. Top with another flounder fillet and slice of smoked salmon. Top with a third flounder fillet. Sprinkle with freshly grated black pepper. Trim edges to make neat packages.

Slice lemons into paper-thin rounds. Place in overlapping slices to cover fish. Wrap tightly in plastic wrap (see Equipment, page 15). Refrigerate for 1 to 2 hours.

Bring a large pot of water, fitted with a flat steamer basket, to a boil. Place wrapped fish in steamer and cover tightly. Steam over boiling water for 10 to 12 minutes until just firm and cooked through. Do not overcook.

Open packages carefully, being careful to reserve all juices. Serve immediately with juices poured over fish.

Serves 4

lemon sole in tomato and preserved lemon sauce

First the lemon: This is a Moroccan condiment you can make at home that lasts and lasts, and for which you'll find a dozen uses. Preserved lemons can also be purchased at Middle Eastern grocery stores. Here the fish is cooked in an uncomplicated sauce of tomato punctuated with bits of preserved lemon rind.

28 ounces canned **plum tomatoes** in thick puree

2 **preserved lemons** in salt (page 14) or store-bought

4 9-ounce fillets of **lemon sole** or flounder

Process tomatoes with puree in bowl of food processor until smooth. Transfer to a large nonstick skillet with a cover and place over medium heat.

Wash preserved lemons thoroughly under cold water. Dry well. Separate wedges, discarding interior flesh. You want to use only the soft rind. Cut rind from 5 wedges into long thin julienned strips. Add to skillet with tomato sauce and stir to distribute. Add a grinding of black pepper and stir again.

Lightly salt both sides of fish. Using a sharp knife, cut fillets in half lengthwise along the center "seam." Place fish fillets side by side in tomato-lemon sauce. Cover skillet and bring to a boil. Immediately lower heat and simmer for 10 minutes.

Transfer fish to platter and keep warm. Bring sauce to a rapid boil and cook for 1 minute, until thickened. Place one piece of fish on each plate, top with some sauce, then top with another piece of fish and finish with sauce. Garnish with a little of the remaining preserved lemon, either finely chopped or julienned. Serve immediately.
Serves 4

miso-glazed grouper, japanese style

Chef Michel Nischan cooks hip, healthy food at New York's Heartbeat, where he shared this 1-2-3 recipe with me. Miso, fermented and aged soybean paste, is used to enrich other foods by providing protein, minerals, and a seductive flavor. Here, *genmai* miso, made of soybeans and brown rice, is diluted with mirin, which is a slightly sweet rice wine; together they impart a "meaty" complexity to firm-textured grouper.

4 tablespoons **miso**, preferably *genmai*

½ cup **mirin** (sweet rice wine)

4 9-ounce fillets of **grouper**, skin removed

Put miso in a small bowl and slowly add mirin, stirring constantly, until a paste is formed. Add freshly ground black pepper and stir.

Rub mixture onto fish fillets to coat completely. Enclose each piece of fish tightly in plastic wrap and refrigerate for 4 to 6 hours.

Preheat broiler.

Unwrap fish, scraping marinade from the plastic wrap and reserving. Make sure there is a thin layer of miso paste remaining on fish. Place fish on a baking sheet sprayed lightly with nonstick vegetable spray. Broil for 4 minutes. Using a pastry brush, brush remaining marinade onto fish and broil for 1 minute longer. Do not overcook.

Remove fish from oven and serve immediately.
Serves 4

next wave tuna salad: tartare and seared

Impeccably fresh fish is essential for my two-way tuna—cold (uncooked) and warm (briefly seared)—for there is no masking of flavor or quality. Only a drizzle of pungent mustard oil and salty capers underscore the clean, sparkling taste, so this is a test of your fishmonger: insist on sushi-grade tuna.

4 tablespoons **mustard oil** (see Note)

2 thick **tuna** steaks, one weighing 1 pound, one weighing ¾ pound

½ cup **capers** in brine

Rub 1 teaspoon mustard oil all over smaller piece of tuna. Season lightly with kosher salt and freshly ground black pepper. Heat a small nonstick skillet until very hot. Add oiled tuna and cook for 1 minute on each side. Inside will be very rare. Set aside to cool.

On an impeccably clean cutting board, dice remaining tuna into ¼-inch cubes. Place in a bowl. Finely chop ¼ cup capers and add to bowl. Add 2 tablespoons mustard oil, 1 tablespoon caper juice, and salt to taste. Mix well.

Pack one-quarter of diced tuna into a 1¼-inch-deep, 2½-inch ring mold to form a "cake" and unmold in the center of a large plate. Repeat with remaining tuna.

Using a very sharp thin-bladed knife, cut seared tuna into 12 thin slices. Place 3 slices around each tuna "cake" like spokes of a wheel. Drizzle with remaining oil and garnish with additional capers.

Serves 4

Note: Mustard oil is available in Middle Eastern food markets and stores specializing in Indian ingredients. Make sure the bottle does not contain an FDA warning "For massage use only " or "for external use only." Choose a brand such as Maya or Palace Foods that contains no erucic acid, or purchase an oil infused with mustard flavor.

lemon-thyme roast chicken with pan juices

low calorie

Perfect roast chicken often tests a great chef's mettle, since we all know that "simple" is hard to do well. Some of the success is up to the chicken, so buy one that's kosher, organic, or free-range. The rest is up to you. Thyme's invigorating aroma not only perfumes the chicken but also your kitchen.

4½-pound **chicken,** kosher, organic, or free-range if possible

3 medium thin-skinned **lemons**

3 large bunches fresh **thyme**

Preheat oven to 375°F.

Remove giblets from chicken. Discard liver, and place giblets in a small saucepan with 2 cups water. Bring to a boil. Lower heat and simmer for 25 minutes. Remove from heat and strain broth through a fine-mesh sieve. Set aside.

Wash chicken and dry well. Using a small sharp knife, make a dozen deep slits in each of two lemons and place in cavity of chicken along with half the fresh thyme. Truss chicken with kitchen string and place in a shallow roasting pan.

Mix 1 teaspoon kosher salt and 2 tablespoons thyme leaves together. Rub mixture all over chicken.

Roast for 1 hour and 20 minutes, basting frequently with pan drippings.

Transfer chicken to a cutting board. Pour off most of the fat from the pan. Add 1 cup broth to the pan and, using a spatula, scrape up browned bits from the pan. Return broth to the saucepan with remaining broth. Add juice of remaining lemon, salt, and freshly ground pepper to taste and bring to a boil. Strain sauce and serve with chicken, carved as desired. Garnish with lemons from cavity, cut into wedges, and additional sprigs of fresh thyme.

Serves 6

chicken velvet salad

low calorie

This energy-saver (of both fuel and effort) is direct from China: a pot of cold water, with a chicken in it, is brought to a boil, and the heat immediately turned off. The pot stays covered (no peeking!) until cooled, about three hours. The resulting chicken is, well, velvet—and truly memorable tossed in delicate Japanese soy sauce and seasoned rice-wine vinegar. Serve ever so slightly warm.

4-pound **chicken**

2 tablespoons Japanese **soy sauce** (shoyu or tamari)

3½ tablespoons seasoned **rice-wine vinegar**

Remove giblets from chicken. Discard or save for another use. Pour 2 tablespoons vinegar in cavity of chicken. Truss chicken with kitchen string.

Place chicken in a covered pot large enough to comfortably accommodate chicken. Cover chicken completely with cold water. Add 3 tablespoons kosher salt and 1 tablespoon whole black pepper-corns. Cover pot and bring to a boil. This will take 15 to 20 minutes. Do not lift cover: listen for the water to boil. Remove pot from heat. Do not lift cover. Let sit for 3½ hours.

Remove chicken and discard skin and all fat. Remove meat from bones, being sure to remove meat from wings as well. Place in a bowl.

Mix shoyu and 1½ tablepoons vinegar together and pour over chicken. Toss lightly, adding salt and freshly ground black pepper to taste, if needed.

Place smaller pieces of chicken on a plate and cover with some thinly sliced breast meat. Serve at room temperature.

Serves 4

chicken and leeks in double-strength sherry consommé

Health-conscious chefs today are serving main courses in broth instead of sauce—a nod to lighter, cleaner flavors. This broth is reduced to its elemental essence, and spiked with sherry. It has all the real and mythical benefits of chicken soup, all the finesse of a four-star meal, and you get the psychic benefit of hands-on cooking.

6-pound roasting **chicken**

2 pounds large **leeks**

3 tablespoons **fino sherry** (see Note)

Preheat oven to 400°F.

Remove giblets from chicken. Wash chicken and dry thoroughly. Discard liver and set giblets aside. Place chicken in a large roasting pan.

Wash leeks. Cut the dark green tops from the leeks and reserve. Remove the roots and discard. Cut three-quarters of the leeks in half lengthwise and wash thoroughly. Cut these leeks in half crosswise and place around the chicken. Season chicken lightly with kosher salt and freshly ground black pepper and place in oven. Roast for about 1 hour and 15 minutes total (about 12 minutes per pound). After 30 minutes of cooking, turn leeks over and add ¼ cup water to pan. Cook for 20 minutes longer and remove leeks. Continue cooking chicken until crisp and golden, about 25 minutes longer.

Remove from oven and transfer chicken to a cutting board. Place roasting pan over high heat and add 1 cup water, using a spatula to scrape up browned bits. Remove from heat and set aside.

Using a sharp knife, cut two sides of breast away from the breast bone and remove each in one whole piece. Cover and set aside. (Or let cool and refrigerate until ready to serve.)

Remove legs and back from chicken and break up carcass. Place carcass, legs, and thighs in a large pot. Add cooked leeks, reserved giblets, 4 quarts cold water (or enough to cover), juices from the roasting pan, 2 teaspoons salt, and pepper. Thinly slice remaining leeks and wash thoroughly. Add to pot.

Bring to a boil uncovered. Lower heat and simmer for 2 hours, periodically skimming off any impurities as they rise to the surface. Adjust heat to maintain a steady simmer.

After 2 hours, remove carcass, legs, and thighs and set aside. Strain soup through a fine-mesh sieve into another large clean pot. Press down firmly to extract all the juices. Discard contents of sieve. Return pot to stove and bring to a boil. You will have about 14 cups. Remove any fat with a large flat spoon as it rises to the top.

Lower heat to medium and cook until broth is reduced to 8 cups, about 1 hour. Add salt to taste at end. (If preparing the day before, remove from heat and let cool. Refrigerate. When ready to serve, remove any fat from surface of soup. Bring to a boil.) Add sherry to taste. Adjust seasonings.

Meanwhile, cut reserved dark green tops of leeks into diamond shapes or fine julienne. Place in a small saucepan with enough water to cover and cook for 2 minutes, until soft. Drain.

Cut reserved cooked chicken breast into thick slices. Remove dark meat from thighs and legs and cut into thick strips. Add to hot consommé and gently heat for 1 to 2 minutes. Divide chicken among 6 large shallow soup bowls. Garnish with cooked dark green leeks. Pour hot soup into bowls (about 1½ cups each) and serve immediately.
Serves 6

Note: Fino is very dry Spanish sherry. You can substitute Amontillado.

cold poached chicken, avocado and mango mousseline

Whip together juicy mango and fleshy avocado and you get a beautiful sauce with intriguing flavor and mousselike texture; you also get antioxidant vitamins C and E, and beta-carotene. Avocados, once a no-no on many diets, are full of beneficial monounsaturated fat.

4 6-ounce skinless, **boneless chicken breasts**

1 very large ripe **mango**, about 1 pound

1 large ripe **avocado**, about ¾ pound

In a large nonstick skillet, bring 2 inches of salted water to a boil. Add chicken breasts and cook over high heat for 2 minutes on one side, turn over and cook for another 2 minutes. Cover pan and lower heat to maintain a simmer. Cook for 2 minutes longer. Remove from heat. Let sit for 5 minutes, covered, or until chicken is just firm to the touch. Remove from water. Wrap in plastic. Chill.

Using a small sharp knife remove skin from mango. Cut flesh away from pit. Cut three-quarters into chunks and put in a blender. Cut avocado in half. Cut one half into chunks and add to blender with a pinch of salt and 1 tablespoon water. Process until very smooth. You will have 1⅓ cups "mousseline" sauce.

Cut chicken into thick slices on the bias, across the width of the breast. Arrange in overlapping slices on serving plates. Sprinkle with salt and freshly ground white pepper. Slice remaining mango quarter and avocado half into thin slices, and use as a garnish. Serve with the sauce spooned over, or under, the chicken. Pass the peppermill at the table.

Serves 4

tandoori chicken on the bone

This Indian preparation, traditionally made in a blazing hot clay oven, or *tandoor*, is so flavorful and moist that it more than compensates for the lack of skin or any visible fat. Tandoori paste, destined to be a twenty-first-century pantry staple, is a knockout spice blend of ginger, garlic, coriander, cumin, and chiles. Yogurt both unites and mellows these flavors.

4 large split **chicken breasts** on the bone, about 12 ounces each

4 tablespoons **tandoori paste** (see Note)

1½ cups plain nonfat **yogurt**

Remove skin from chicken breasts. Make 3 slashes in each breast and rub the surface thoroughly with 1 tablespoon tandoori paste for each breast, making sure the paste gets into the cut flesh.

Roll breasts in yogurt to coat. Cover and refrigerate for 6 to 8 hours.

Preheat oven to 400°F. Remove breasts from marinade.

Lightly coat baking sheet with nonstick vegetable spray. Place breasts on baking sheet. Bake for 22 to 25 minutes, until just firm to the touch. Do not overcook.

Sprinkle lightly with kosher salt and serve immediately.

Serves 4

Note: Tandoori paste is available in many supermarkets and specialty food stores. I like the Pataks brand.

sautéed chicken breasts with oven-dried grapes

Looking like a professional chef-made demi-glace, this remarkable sauce is actually made from grapes. Grapes contain flavonoids, protective phytochemicals that are purported to reduce risk of heart disease and some kinds of cancer. When oven-dried, grapes shrivel and add tiny explosions of intense flavor to low-fat chicken.

1½ pounds seedless **grapes**: ¾ pound red, ¾ pound green

3½ tablespoons unsalted **butter**, chilled

4 6-ounce skinless, **boneless chicken breasts**

Preheat oven to 275°F.

Wash grapes and remove from stems. Set aside half of red and green grapes. Place remaining grapes on a baking sheet and bake for 1½ hours, shaking pan frequently. Remove from oven and set aside.

Place uncooked grapes in a blender and puree until very smooth. Strain through a coarse-mesh sieve, pressing down hard on the skins. You will have about ¾ cup juice.

In a large nonstick skillet, melt 2 tablespoons butter. Season chicken with kosher salt and freshly ground black pepper. Add to pan and cook over medium-high heat for 5 minutes on each side, until golden.

Add grape juice and cook for 5 minutes longer, or until chicken is done, and is just firm to the touch. Be careful not to overcook. The grape juices will darken into a mahogany-colored sauce. Transfer breasts to a platter.

Add remaining 1½ tablespoons butter to pan and cook over high heat for 1 minute. Add oven-dried grapes and cook for 1 minute longer. Add salt and pepper to taste and pour sauce over chicken. Serve immediately.

Serves 4

chicken chaud-froid with yogurt-lime glaze

Something unexpected occurs when chicken marinates in yogurt and lime juice: a shiny coating forms and sets when baked, looking a lot like classic *chaud-froid*—a French dish that is prepared hot, but glazed with aspic and served cold.

2 cups plain low-fat **yogurt**

4 large **limes**

4 8-ounce skinless, **boneless chicken breasts**

Put yogurt in a cheesecloth-lined coarse-mesh sieve with a bowl underneath to catch liquid. Let sit unrefrigerated for 1 hour. Discard liquid.

Grate rind of limes to yield 2 teaspoons zest. Add to yogurt. Squeeze 2 limes to yield 3½ tablespoons lime juice. Add to yogurt with ½ teaspoon kosher salt and freshly ground black pepper. Stir well and pour over chicken. Cover and refrigerate for 2 hours.

Preheat oven to 400°F.

Lift chicken from yogurt, making sure the surface is lightly coated. Place on a baking sheet. Bake for 10 to 12 minutes, until cooked through. Remove from oven and transfer to a plate. Let cool. Chill until ready to serve.

Thinly slice remaining limes and serve alongside chicken.

Serves 4

red hens with sumac and shallots

Ruddy sumac, ground from berries of a Mediterranean shrub, has a mysteriously tart flavor and tints these little hens red. The juice and pulp of grated shallots act as a tenderizing marinade and, when sliced, they become a flavorful bed on which the hens can roast.

2 1¼-pound **poussins** (baby chickens) or small cornish hens

10 large **shallots**

⅓ cup ground **sumac** (see Note)

Have the butcher butterfly the poussins for you or do it yourself: with kitchen shears, cut poussins along the length of the backbone; cut out backbone; turn poussins over so that breast is facing you and pound flat, using your fist.

Peel 2 shallots. Grate them on the large holes of a box grater. Rub grated shallots and juices all over chicken. Sprinkle lightly with kosher salt and freshly ground black pepper. Wrap and refrigerate for 4 to 6 hours.

Preheat oven to 400°F.

Peel remaining shallots and slice very thin. Unwrap poussins and scrape off shallots. Pat poussins dry using paper towels. Sprinkle 1 table-

spoon sumac on each poussin to coat thoroughly.

Place 2 poussins, skin side up, on each of 2 rimmed baking sheets. Place mounds of shallots under each poussin so that each poussin is sitting on a bed of shallots. Roast for 35 to 40 minutes, until the juices run clear.

Cut poussins in half lengthwise through the breast and serve with shallots. Sprinkle plate lightly with remaining sumac.

Serves 4

Note: Ground sumac is available in Middle Eastern food stores and spice markets.

turkey salad with grape tomatoes and zucchini, zucchini coulis

low calorie & low fat

A vibrantly colored still-life: plump white chunks of succulent turkey, the reddest grape tomatoes, and a vivid green sauce fashioned from simply cooked fresh zucchini. Careful poaching and impeccable ingredients are integral to this dish's success.

2 **turkey "tenderloins"** about 1½ pounds

8 ounces **grape tomatoes**, about 32

4 medium **zucchini**, about 1½ pounds

Season tenderloins with kosher salt and finely ground white pepper. Wrap each in plastic wrap (see Equipment, page 15), making sure to create an airtight package. You can steam them in a steamer basket or poach them, double-wrapped, in a shallow pan of boiling water.

To steam: Bring a pot of water to a boil. Fit with a steamer basket. Place tenderloins in basket and cover. Cook for 14 minutes. Turn off heat. Let sit, covered, for 5 minutes, then remove from steamer. Let cool in plastic. Refrigerate until cold. Cut turkey into ½-inch chunks.

To poach: Fill a 10-inch skillet with several inches of water. Bring to a boil. Carefully add plastic-wrapped tenderloins. Lower heat to medium. Cook for 6 minutes on each side. Turn off heat. Let sit in water for 6 minutes. Remove from water. Let cool in plastic. Refrigerate until cold. Cut turkey into ½-inch chunks.

To make zucchini coulis: Wash 2 zucchini and cut into thick rounds. Cut rounds in half and place in a small saucepan. Add enough salted water to just cover. Bring to a boil. Lower heat and cover. Cook for 15 minutes, until very soft

Using a slotted spoon, transfer zucchini to a blender. Add ½ to ⅔ cup cooking water. Process until very smooth. Add kosher salt and freshly ground black pepper to taste. Chill until ready to serve.

To assemble salad: Divide turkey equally among 4 large plates. Slice 1 zucchini into paper-thin slices and place around turkey. Wash tomatoes and cut in half lengthwise, saving several to cut into rounds to place atop zucchini circles. Tuck halved tomatoes among pieces of turkey. Cut remaining zucchini into thin slices and tuck in among tomatoes. Pour zucchini coulis over turkey and serve.

Serves 4

HEALTHY 1-2-3 [93]

rolled and tied turkey roast with fresh sage and baked pears

I love this cut of turkey, which most butchers carry. Half of a plump turkey breast with skin on and bones removed, looks like, and can be used like, London broil. But in this recipe it's stuffed with sage, whose essential oils have antiseptic properties and a reputation for promoting circulation. Pears, especially aromatic Anjou pears, become a delectable sauce and a fiber-rich accompaniment. This can also be prepared without skin to further reduce calories and fat.

2 large bunches **sage**

2¼-pound **turkey** "London broil," ½ breast with all bones removed

3 large ripe **Anjou pears**

Preheat oven to 400°F.

Chop enough sage leaves to yield ¼ cup. Place in a blender with ½ teaspoon kosher salt, 2 tablespoons water, and freshly ground black pepper to taste. Process until the mixture becomes a paste. If this is difficult because of the small amount, turn mixture out onto a chopping board and finely mince. You should have 2 tablespoons paste.

Place turkey, skin-side down, on a board. Spread sage paste on flesh of turkey breast. Lengthwise, roll turkey breast to make a cylindrical shape, about 10 inches long by 4 inches wide at the widest point in the center. Tie with kitchen string at 1½-inch intervals. Season turkey with salt and pepper. Tuck whole sage leaves under the strings to cover top.

Peel pears and cut in half lengthwise. Remove seeds.

Place turkey in a shallow roasting pan. Place pears, cut side down, around turkey.

Bake turkey for 45 to 50 minutes, until it registers 150°F on a meat thermometer. Place under broiler for 1 minute, until skin browns a little and sage leaves are crisp. Transfer turkey and pears to a carving board.

Pour ½ cup boiling water into roasting pan over medium-high heat and scrape up any browned bits. Pour roasting juices into a blender with 3 pear halves that have been cut into pieces. Puree until very smooth. Strain through a coarse-mesh sieve. Add salt and pepper to taste. Cut remaining pears in half lengthwise. Slice turkey as desired. Serve with pear sauce, pear quarters, and fresh sage leaves.

Serves 6

duck magret with roasted red onions and pomegranate molasses

Should duck strike you as too fatty or too complicated, here's a gorgeous 1-2-3 recipe. You need just a bit of rendered fat (purported to be of the healthy sort) to sauté succulent duck breasts. The syrup of pomegranates, rich in taste and mythology, adds tart-sweet synergy. Onions, grated raw, tenderize the duck and, when roasted, are transformed into a robust vegetable accompaniment.

4 11-ounce boned **duck breasts** with skin (to be removed later)

3 large oval-shaped **red onions**

5 tablespoons **pomegranate molasses**, plus more for drizzling (see Note)

Cut duck breasts in half to get 8 lobes. Remove skin from each lobe. Save skin from 1 lobe (about 2 ounces) and discard the rest.

Place duck breasts in a large bowl. Peel 1 onion and cut in half through the root end. Grate on the large holes of a box grater to yield ½ cup grated onion. Add to duck breasts along with 5 tablespoons pomegranate molasses and freshly ground black pepper to taste. Mix thoroughly. Cover and refrigerate for 2 to 3 hours.

About 1½ hours before serving, preheat oven to 350°F. Cut remaining 2 onions in half lengthwise through the root end. In a small nonstick skillet heat one-quarter of reserved duck skin for several minutes until about 1 tablespoon fat is rendered. Coat cut sides of onions with duck fat. Place onions, cut side down, on a rimmed baking sheet or in a metal pie tin and roast for 1½ hours, turning onions over after 1 hour.

About 15 minutes before serving, remove duck breasts from marinade, scraping off and reserving marinade. In each of 2 large nonstick skillets cook half of remaining skin so that 1 tablespoon is rendered in each pan. When duck fat is hot, add breasts that have been lightly sprinkled with kosher salt and cook over medium-high heat for about 3 minutes on each side. Add some of the reserved marinade and 1 tablespoon water to each pan and cook for 1 minute. Remove duck breasts to cutting board. Let rest for 1 minute. Remove onions from oven, removing any skin. Place a roasted onion in center of each of 4 large plates. Cut breasts on the bias into ¼-inch-thick slices. Surround onion with overlapping slices of duck. Drizzle with pan juices. Serve immediately.
Serves 4

Note: Pomegranate molasses is available in Middle Eastern and specialty food markets.

brined pork loin with orange-chipotle jus

Soaking pork in salt water keeps it incredibly moist and flavorful, but not perceptibly salty. Triple Sec, an orange-based spirit, sweetens the heat of smoky chipotle peppers.

1½-pound boneless **pork loin**, tied at ½-inch intervals

¼ cup plus 2 tablespoons **Triple Sec**

3 canned **chipotle peppers** in adobo sauce, including 1½ teaspoons of the sauce

In a large bowl, put 8 cups water and ¼ cup kosher salt and stir to dissolve. Add pork loin, making sure pork is covered. If not, add water. Cover and refrigerate for 4 to 6 hours. Remove pork from brine and pat dry.

Place ¼ cup Triple Sec and 3 coarsely chopped chipotle peppers with about 1 teaspoon adobo sauce in a small saucepan. Add a large pinch of salt and bring to a boil. Lower heat to medium-high and cook for 2 minutes. The marinade will be thick and syrupy. Let cool.

Place pork loin in a shallow casserole. Spread chipotle marinade over meat, making sure to coat all sides. Cover and refrigerate for 3 to 4 hours.

Preheat oven to 400°F.

Lift pork loin from marinade and place on a rimmed baking sheet. Reserve marinade and set aside. Roast pork loin for 35 minutes, until it reaches an internal temperature of 140°F, then place under broiler for 1 minute. Transfer pork to a cutting board and let rest while you prepare sauce. Add ½ cup boiling water to the baking sheet and scrape up browned bits. Strain roasting juices through a fine-mesh sieve into a small saucepan. Add reserved marinade and 2 tablespoons Triple Sec. Bring to a boil and cook for 1 minute. Add salt to taste.

Sprinkle salt on pork and cut pork into ⅓-inch-thick slices, adding any accumulated juices to the saucepan. Add remaining ½ teaspoon adobo, if you like it spicy. Serve immediately with orange-chipotle jus.

Serves 4

pork tenderloin with sweet mustard and rosemary

The ancient Greeks and Romans knew the culinary and medicinal gifts of mustard, which in this recipe forms a protective and flavorful coating for pork tenderloin, an excellent source of B vitamins. In classical Greece and Rome, rosemary, too, was valued in both medicine and cooking.

2 12-ounce **pork tenderloins**

½ cup plus 2 tablespoons good-quality **honey mustard** (see Note)

1 large bunch fresh **rosemary**

Remove any fat from tenderloins.

In a small bowl, mix mustard with 2 tablespoons finely minced rosemary needles. Add a grinding of black pepper. Pour mustard mixture over tenderloins and roll tenderloins so they are completely coated. Cover and refrigerate for 4 to 6 hours.

Preheat oven to 375°F.

Remove most of the marinade from pork. Season lightly with kosher salt and freshly ground black pepper. Distribute rosemary branches in center of a baking sheet, placing tenderloins on top. Bake for 12 minutes, turn over, and bake 12 minutes longer. Remove from oven. Transfer to a cutting board and let rest for 5 minutes. Pork should be slightly pink. Slice thinly, placing pork in overlapping slices on a serving platter. Pour accumulated juices over pork. Garnish with sprigs of rosemary and add a dollop of honey mustard.
Serves 4

Note: I use Honeycup or Sable & Rosenfeld.

potted leeks and corned beef in riesling

This eccentric combination of ingredients gives off a fabulous bouquet that will have your mouth watering. You get a rich broth sweetened with leeks, perfumed by Riesling and accented with salty, pickled corned beef drippings. Emperor Nero considered leeks good for vocal chords, and ate them regularly in order to sing for his supper.

6 large **leeks**

2¼ pounds **corned beef,** in one piece

1 750-ml bottle dry **Riesling**

Cut roots off leeks. Trim 2 inches from green tops of leeks and discard. Split leeks in half, lengthwise, and wash thoroughly, making sure to wash between the leaves.

Lay half the leeks in bottom of a very large non-reactive pot or Dutch oven with cover. Place corned beef on top. Cover with remaining leeks.

Pour Riesling into pot. Add 3 cups water and ½ tablespoon whole black peppercorns. Bring to a boil. Lower heat and simmer for 2½ hours or until tender.

Transfer meat to a cutting board. Cut across the grain into thin slices with a sharp thin-bladed knife.

Place some leeks in 6 large shallow soup bowls. Add equally portioned slices of corned beef on top, and top with more leeks. Pour ½ cup hot broth over meat. Serve immediately, sprinkled with a few grains of coarse sea salt.
Serves 6

cumin-crusted lamb with apricots

These flavors and aromas transport me to Marrakesh, where our friend Latif, son of the late imam of the great mosque there, guided us through the bustling and mysterious spice markets. Here's how I've recaptured the memory: A boned leg of lamb is stuffed with intensely flavored dried apricots, high in beta-carotene and potassium, then rubbed with aromatic cumin. Buy your cumin from a Middle Eastern market or spice store for the most flavorful results.

7-pound leg of **lamb,** boned and butterflied by the butcher (net weight about 4¼ pounds)

¼ cup ground **cumin**

½ pound large good-quality **dried apricots**

Preheat oven to 400°F.

Remove all visible fat from the lamb.

In a small skillet, put cumin powder plus 2 teaspoons kosher salt. Heat over medium heat for 1 to 2 minutes, stirring frequently, until the aroma rises. Let cool.

Place apricots in a bowl. Pour boiling water over apricots to cover. Let sit for 15 minutes to plump. Drain thoroughly.

Open lamb and place on a work surface so that it remains flat. Sprinkle lamb with half the cumin-salt mixture and freshly ground black pepper.

Place drained apricots in a long, overlapping row, lengthwise down the center of the lamb. Roll lamb tightly around the apricot filling. Using heavy string, tie roast at 1-inch intervals.

Rub roast with remaining cumin-salt mixture. Sprinkle with freshly ground black pepper.

Coat a large shallow roasting pan with nonstick vegetable spray. Place roast in pan. Roast for 1 hour and 20 minutes, or until meat thermometer reads 135°F for medium-rare.

Remove roast from oven. Place on a large cutting board and let rest for 10 minutes. Meanwhile, in a small saucepan bring 2 cups water to a boil. Pour off almost all the fat from the roasting pan and pour in the boiling water, scraping up browned bits. Strain through a fine-mesh sieve into saucepan.

Carve lamb into thick slices. Add any juices from board to saucepan. Heat briefly, adding salt and pepper to taste. Pour over lamb.
Serves 10

lamb chops provençal

Chops cut from the shoulder are a bourgeois alternative to the more familiar—and pricier—loin or rib lamb chops. But when crusted in herbes de Provence, they become decidedly chic.

¼ cup **herbes de Provence** (see Note)

4 large **lemons**

4 10-ounce thick shoulder **lamb chops** on the bone

Place herbes de Provence in a small bowl. Grate the rind of 1 or 2 lemons to yield 1 tablespoon zest. Add to herbs along with 2 teaspoons kosher salt. Mix well.

Place lamb chops in a shallow casserole. Squeeze the juice of ½ lemon over each lamb chop. Let sit for 20 minutes, turn over and let sit for 20 minutes longer.

Preheat oven to 475°F.

Pack herb mixture onto 1 side of each lamb chop to cover completely. Tie chops with string 1 inch in from each end. Place chops, herb side up, on a baking sheet.

Bake for 15 minutes. Turn over and bake for 5 minutes longer.

Remove string. Serve herb side up with wedges of remaining lemons.

Serves 4

Note: Herbes de Provence, available in specialty food stores, is a mixture that includes dried lavender, thyme, rosemary, basil, marjoram, and savory.

rib-eye roast, gravlax-style

In this unusual preparation, the beef is cured overnight in dill, sugar, salt, and pepper, a Nordic preparation usually reserved for salmon, and then roasted. The result? Extraordinarily tender and rosy slices of flavorful meat. Fresh dill may settle the stomach, which is a good thing if you're tempted to over-indulge.

3½-pound **rib-eye roast**, rolled and tied (about 6½ inches long and 5 inches in diameter)

2 large bunches fresh **dill**, enough to yield about 1½ cups

3 tablespoons **sugar**

Pat beef dry with a paper towel.

Wash the dill and dry thoroughly. Finely chop dill leaves to yield 1 cup, firmly packed. Save remaining dill for garnish.

Mix sugar, ¼ cup kosher salt, and 1 teaspoon coarsely ground black pepper in a small bowl. Coat all sides of meat with this mixture, rubbing it into the surface of the roast. Pat chopped dill on top, bottom, and sides of roast. Wrap tightly in plastic wrap.

Place beef in a small roasting pan and weight down with a baking sheet topped with several heavy cans, or with a water-filled teapot. Place in refrigerator and marinate for 18 to 24 hours, but no longer.

When ready to cook, remove roast from refrigerator and remove plastic wrap. Preheat oven to 400°F. Let roast sit at room temperature for 30 minutes.

Scrape all the dill and all the spice mixture from roast. Place roast in a shallow, heavy roasting pan. Cook for about 1 hour and 15 minutes, or until a meat thermometer reaches 130°F for rare to medium-rare.

Remove from oven. Transfer meat to a cutting board and let rest for 5 minutes.

Carve meat into ½-inch-thick slices and garnish with remaining sprigs of dill.

Serves 10

boeuf à la ficelle with shiitakes and ginger

This is fusion cooking at its best: a French preparation with Asian undercurrents. Fillet of beef is poached until rare while suspended from a wooden spoon in a beneficent broth of shiitake mushrooms and ginger. The broth is then reduced to a new version of old-fashioned "beef tea," some of which is poured over the sliced meat. Asian cultures have long respected the health attributes of shiitakes, believed to help reduce serum cholesterol and enhance immunity, and ginger, believed to be a powerful anti-inflammatory.

4-inch piece fresh **ginger**

1¼ ounces large **dried shiitake mushrooms**

2-pound **fillet of beef**

In a large oval pot put 4½ quarts water. Peel ginger and cut in half crosswise. Then cut into long paper-thin slices. Add sliced ginger and shiitakes to pot along with 15 whole black peppercorns and 1 tablespoon kosher salt. Bring to a boil, lower heat, and simmer for 20 minutes.

Tie beef with a string so that the string wraps around length and width of beef (as if you were tying a ribbon around a present). Attach a small bow or loop where the strings cross and stick the handle of a long wooden spoon through the loop.

Gently place beef in simmering broth, placing the spoon on opposite rims of the pot. You want the beef suspended in the broth and not touching the bottom or sides of pot, so that the broth cooks all of the meat evenly. Broth should cover beef. Add additional water, if necessary, to cover.

Cover pot, letting lid rest on spoon, and cook gently for 25 to 30 minutes, or until a meat thermometer reads 125°F. Transfer beef to a cutting board. Let rest for 10 minutes. Meanwhile, pour 4 cups shiitake stock through a fine-mesh sieve lined with rinsed cheesecloth into a saucepan. Bring to a boil and cook until reduced to 3 cups.

Sprinkle meat with salt and pepper. Cut into ½-inch-thick slices and place in large shallow soup bowls or on large dinner plates. Garnish with shiitake mushrooms retrieved from the pot and a little of the cooked ginger. Pour ½ cup broth over beef. Serve immediately. Save remaining broth for other uses (making soups or drinking as a restorative "beef tea").

Serves 6 or more

Orange, Black Olive, and Mint Salad • Caçik (Turkish

ets, Balsamic Syrup and Crispy Greens • Steamed

• Broccoli di Rape with Sultanas • Brussels Sprouts

tinée with Prosciutto • Cipolle al Forno • Steamed

with Aged Tamari • Raspberry-Kissed Red Cabbage

eur • Poached Leeks with Roasted Garlic and Brie

pers, Za'atar Oil • Petite Ratatouille • Apples and

Onion Cups • Julienned Snow Peas with Lemon Oil

Butter • Summer Squash with Fresh Basil • Vibrant

e • Rosemary-Roasted Turnips • Yucca Puree with

Spinach with Toasted Pistachios • Baked Potatoes

es • Snow Peas in the French Style • Crisp Cumin

: Hot Vegetable and Cold Dip •Tiny Lentils with Port-

White Beans in Pesto • Bulghur with Morels and Dried

Oil • Little Tomato-Pesto "Napoleons" • Polenta with

roth • Frenched String Beans with Sweet Garlic Sauce

vegetables and side dishes

Prior to the year zero, Confucius and his contemporary Lao-Tse

sought harmony with natural foods, plants, and herbs. Concerned with nutritional values, Lao-Tse (who founded Taoism) was the first to advocate eating vegetables raw or only partially cooked.

With a two-millennium divide between us, evidence again proclaims that diets rich in vegetables, salads, and fresh fruits can significantly reduce the risks of heart disease and cancer. Phytochemicals, which are found in abundance in these foods, help individual cells in the body to function properly, so much depends on plant matter: your natural defenses rely on the variety and nutritional quality of your food.

The famous—and valid—mandate of nutritionists is to "eat all the colors," and I've tried to follow that here: vibrant green spinach-fennel puree, bright yellow summer squash with basil, raspberry-kissed red cabbage, and a sunny orange confit of carrots and lemon, are just a few. Only small adornments are suggested: a sprig of fragrant herb, a drizzle of heart-healthy olive oil, a dot of butter, a crunchy sprinkle of mineral-rich sea salt.

To enlighten the palate, I suggest using organic vegetables whenever possible because they just taste better, pure and simple. Nearly all of this chapter's recipes are vegetarian, and a significant number are dairy-free. Fitting neatly into many healthy-eating plans, they only begin to scratch the surface of this generous earth.

After generations of breeding vegetables primarily to survive long hauls to supermarkets, the worm (in this country) is starting to turn. A new age of produce is here, and it looks

something like an older age, when growers and consumers were more interdependent. The

movement to replant heirlooms, our ancestors' varieties of vegetables and fruits; the

growth of organic farms across the country; new systems of sustainable agriculture;

respect for plants' seasons; and a devotion to quality and nutrition will, if not overwhelmed

by biotechnology, at least give us alternative choices in the years ahead.

Once the domain of health food stores alone, organic fruits, grains, and vegetables are

available, thankfully, in many chain supermarkets. Selecting them reduces the use of pes-

ticides in our ecosystem—so you're helping your community as well as your body.

little uncooked salads

These little salads represent my 1-2-3 philosophy of letting ingredients speak for themselves by manipulating them as little as possible. They should also appeal to New Age eaters who "shop close to the ground" by consuming as many raw foods as possible. The tastes are direct and refreshing; two or three would make a lovely antipasto.

grated carrot–citrus salad

3 large **carrots**

4 tablespoons fresh **lemon juice**

1 tablespoon **orange-flower water** (see Note)

Peel carrots. Grate on large holes of box grater. Place in a bowl. Toss with lemon juice, orange-flower water, and kosher salt and freshly ground black pepper to taste. Marinate for at least 1 hour. Best served at room temperature for optimum fragrance and taste.

Serves 4

Note: Orange-flower water is a distillate of bitter orange flowers, available in small blue bottles in Middle Eastern and specialty food shops.

yellow tomato salsa

3 large ripe yellow **tomatoes**

1 clove **garlic**, peeled

1 small bunch **basil**

Wash tomatoes and core. Cut as meticulously as possible into ¼-inch cubes. Place in a bowl. Push garlic through a garlic press. Add to tomatoes.

Wash basil leaves and chop very finely to yield ⅓ cup. Toss with tomatoes along with coarse sea salt and freshly ground black pepper. Marinate for 30 minutes before serving.

Serves 4

low calorie & fat-free

low calorie & fat-free

shaved fennel with parmesan

1 large **fennel** bulb, about 1½ pounds

3½ tablespoons **white balsamic vinegar**

3-ounce piece **Parmigiano-Reggiano**

Trim the feathery fronds from the fennel bulb and set aside. Remove any brown spots and trim root end. Slice fennel as thinly as possible, cutting through the root end. Place in a bowl.

Add vinegar, and fine sea salt and freshly ground black pepper to taste. Break cheese into very small pieces and add to salad. Toss again. Let sit for 1 hour before serving.

Scatter finely chopped fennel fronds on top.

Serves 4

blood orange, black olive, and mint salad

8 **blood oranges**

20 **kalamata olives**

1 small bunch **mint**

Using a small sharp knife, cut rind from oranges, making sure to remove white pith. Slice oranges into thin rounds, less than ¼ inch thick. Remove any seeds. Place on a platter with any accumulated juice. Cut each olive into 4 pieces, slicing panels away from the pit. Scatter on the oranges. Cut mint into fine julienne and scatter on the salad. Marinate for at least 30 minutes before serving.

Serves 4

caçik (turkish cucumbers)

2 medium **cucumbers**

1 teaspoon **Asian sesame oil**

1 cup plain **nonfat plain yogurt**

Peel cucumbers. Cut in half lengthwise and remove the seeds, using a small spoon. Slice into ¼-inch-thick "half-moons." Place in a bowl. Add oil, yogurt, and kosher salt and freshly ground black pepper to taste. Stir and refrigerate for 1 to 2 hours.

Serves 4

jicama with lime and cilantro

low calorie & fat-free

1 large **jicama**, about 1½ pounds

2 large **limes**

1 small bunch **cilantro**

Using a small sharp knife, peel jicama. Cut into matchsticks ⅛-inch thick by 3-inches long. Place in a bowl and add the juice of 1 lime and about 3 to 4 tablespoons finely chopped cilantro, as desired.

Add kosher salt and freshly ground black pepper to taste. Refrigerate for 30 minutes or longer. Serve cold with additional lime, cut into wedges.
Serves 4

radish raita

low calorie & low fat

In India, raitas are cucumber-yogurt salads traditionally eaten with spicy curries to refresh the palate. Here I've substituted radishes, which have their own interesting history: They once were considered so valuable that pharaohs used them to pay the pyramid builders. Along with their virtuous leaves (cooked for a brief minute), they provide color, texture, and vitamins.

1 large bunch large **radishes**, with leaves

2 cups plain low-fat **yogurt**

1 clove **garlic**, peeled

Wash radishes and radish leaves well. Dry thoroughly. Remove leaves and reserve. Discard stems and radish roots.

Slice radishes into thin rounds. Place in a bowl and add yogurt. Mix well. Bring a small pot of salted water to a boil. Add radish leaves and blanch for 1 minute. Drain under cold water and squeeze dry. Chop coarsely and add to bowl with yogurt.

Push garlic through a press. Add kosher salt and freshly ground black pepper to taste. Mix well and refrigerate for 1 hour before serving.
Serves 4 or more

warm roasted beets, balsamic syrup and crispy greens

A syrup of reduced balsamic vinegar adds its own sweetness to the slow-roasted beets and a pleasant sour nip for balance. But this dish's best feature is its unexpected flourish of beet greens, crisped to airy perfection. They disappear like snowflakes on your tongue.

3 large bunches **beets** with leaves, about 4 pounds (10 to 12 beets)

1½ cups **balsamic vinegar**

3 cloves **garlic**, peeled

Preheat oven to 300°F.

Cut stems and leaves from beets. Reserve for later use. Cut off root ends of beets and discard. Wash beets, scrubbing thoroughly. Place in oven directly on the rack and roast for 2½ to 3 hours, or until tender when pierced with the tip of a sharp knife. If you'd rather use a baking sheet, make sure it is nonstick or lined with foil.

Wash beet leaves well and dry thoroughly. Chop finely. Place on a baking sheet and bake at 300°F for 20 to 30 minutes, or until crisp. Turn once or twice during baking. When crisp, remove from oven, sprinkle with kosher salt, and set aside.

Meanwhile, place balsamic vinegar in a small saucepan and cook over medium-high heat until reduced to ¾ cup, about 15 to 20 minutes. Vinegar will become syrupy.

When beets are tender, remove from oven. Peel beets. Cut half of the beets into thick slices and the other half into wedges.

Finely mince garlic. Pour warm vinegar over hot beets and toss with garlic. Top with crispy leaves and toss again.

Serves 6

steamed asparagus with wasabi butter

Want to make a Frenchman gasp? When the revered asparagus first break the soil in early spring, Gallic taste calls for a classic vinaigrette or a quick sauté in butter. I've added a jolt of wasabi, commonly referred to as Japanese horseradish, for zippier flavor.

4 tablespoons unsalted **butter**, at room temperature

2 teaspoons **wasabi powder**

2 pounds medium **asparagus**

Cut butter into ½-inch pieces and place in the bowl of an electric mixer. Mix wasabi with 1 teaspoon water and add to butter. Add a pinch of kosher salt. Mix until wasabi is thoroughly incorporated. Scrape out mixture and place in a small bowl. Refrigerate until cold.

Snap off woody bottoms of asparagus. With a vegetable peeler, peel bottoms of asparagus stalks, using a light hand. Fill a 10-inch skillet with several inches of water. Add ½ tablespoon kosher salt. Bring to a boil. Add asparagus and cook for about 10 minutes, until stalks are easily pierced with the tip of a sharp knife. They should still be bright green. Do not overcook. Drain thoroughly.

Divide asparagus into 6 equal portions and arrange on individual plates or place on a platter. Divide wasabi butter into 6 portions. Place on asparagus. Sprinkle with salt and coarsely ground black pepper. Serve immediately.

Serves 6

stir-fried asparagus with tofu

Made from nutritional-powerhouse soybeans, tofu has many virtues: It is a highly concentrated protein; it is a source of calcium; it can activate toxin-destroying enzymes; and it is so bland and malleable that you can do almost anything to it. Here I've cut little cubes from a block of tofu and then crisped them to mimic croutons (while keeping their insides creamy).

1¼ pounds medium **asparagus**

5-ounce block firm **tofu**

1 tablespoon plus 2 teaspoons **roasted peanut oil** (see Note)

Snap off woody bottoms of asparagus. With a vegetable peeler, peel bottoms of asparagus stalks, using a light hand. Cut asparagus on the bias into 1½-inch lengths.

Carefully cut tofu into ⅓-inch cubes.

Heat oil in a wok or a nonstick skillet until hot. Add asparagus and tofu. Stir-fry over high heat for 5 to 6 minutes, stirring often. Adjust heat. Cook until asparagus is browned and caramelized and the tofu is golden and crisp.

Add sea salt and freshly ground black pepper to taste. Serve immediately.
Serves 4

Note: Use roasted, not plain, peanut oil for optimal flavor. It is available in many supermarkets and health-food stores.

broccoli-ginger puree

Broccoli may be a girl's best friend: It is a good source of calcium and vitamin K for bones and thousands of protective phytochemicals. When coupled with the cholesterol-reducing powers of ginger, it is unusually delicious and nutritious.

4-inch piece fresh **ginger**

1½ heads **broccoli,** about 2 pounds

4 ½ tablespoons **heavy cream**

Peel ginger with a small sharp knife, then grate on large holes of box grater. Put grated ginger in a paper towel and squeeze juice into a small cup. You will have about 1½ tablespoons juice. Set aside.

Bring a large pot of salted water to a boil. Cut stems from broccoli, peel, and cut into small pieces. Cut remaining broccoli into florets.

Add stems to boiling water and cook over medium heat for 5 minutes. Add florets and cook for 8 minutes more, or until broccoli is tender but still bright green.

Drain broccoli in a colander and place in bowl of a food processor. Process into small pieces. With the motor running, add ginger juice and cream. Process until very smooth. Add kosher salt and freshly ground black pepper to taste.

When ready to serve, heat puree in a saucepan, adding a little water if too thick. Serve immediately.

Serves 6

broccoli di rape with sultanas

Broccoli di rape, also known as broccoli rabe or raab, and cime di rape in Italy, comes in bunches of thin stalks with green leaves and tight little green buds. Some people find this more tender relative of broccoli too bitter, so I've teamed it here with sweet sultanas for contrast. Sultanas, or golden raisins, are green grapes that have been dried; rich in minerals, they are sweet bursts in a tangle of bitter greens.

1½ pounds **broccoli di rape**

1½ cups fat-free **chicken broth**

½ cup **sultanas** or golden raisins

Trim the tough bottoms, about ½-inch, from broccoli di rape. Wash thoroughly and dry. Place in a large skillet with the broth and sultanas. Bring to a boil, lower heat, and cook until tender, about 15 to 18 minutes.

Remove broccoli di rape and sultanas with tongs, letting excess liquid drain off. Quickly cook broth over high heat until it's reduced by half. Add freshly ground black pepper and pour over hot broccoli di rape. Serve immediately.

Serves 4

brussels sprouts with orange-balsamic reduction

Brussels sprouts deserve more respect, since their bad reputation, like that of cabbage, comes from relentless overcooking. A cruciferous vegetable, they contain many compounds that may strengthen the immune system. Behind their mild pungency is a subtle sweetness that's brought out by the addition of fresh orange juice and balsamic vinegar.

1 pound **Brussels sprouts**

6 large juice **oranges**

3 tablespoons **balsamic vinegar**

Wash Brussels sprouts and trim bottoms. Cut in half through the stem end.

Using a small sharp knife or vegetable peeler, cut rind from 1 orange. Set aside.

Cut oranges in half and squeeze to get 2 cups juice. Add 2 tablespoons balsamic vinegar to juice and stir.

Place Brussels sprouts in one layer in a large skillet. Pour orange juice mixture over Brussels sprouts and bring to a boil. Cover pan and cook over low heat for 15 to 20 minutes, until tender.

Meanwhile, remove any pith from reserved orange rind and cut into very fine julienne. Boil in a small pot of water for 1 minute. Drain and set aside.

Remove Brussels sprouts with slotted spoon and put in a bowl. Add remaining tablespoon vinegar to pan juices and cook over high heat until reduced and syrupy. Pour over hot Brussels sprouts, adding kosher salt and freshly ground black pepper to taste. Garnish with blanched orange rind. Serve hot.

Serves 4

butternut squash–tangerine puree

Butternut, a winter squash, is richer in nutrients than its summer relatives. Its flesh is full of fiber and its orange color tells you there's lots of beta-carotene. Tangerines, which disappear into the squash's strong color, add a mysterious background flavor as well as a blast of vitamin C.

2 medium **butternut squash**, about 3½ pounds

4 **tangerines**

3 tablespoons unsalted **butter**

Preheat oven to 400°F.

Cut squash in half, lengthwise, then cut each piece in half crosswise. Remove seeds and membranes. Place in a rimmed baking pan, cut side down, and pour in ⅓ cup water. Bake for 1 hour, turning over after 40 minutes. Squash will be lightly caramelized.

Meanwhile, cut 2 tangerines in half and squeeze to get ⅓ to ½ cup juice. Peel remaining tangerines. Cut away any white membrane and

separate into segments. Dice tangerines into small pieces.

Remove squash from oven. Remove flesh from skin, using a spoon. Place in a food processor with butter and enough tangerine juice to make a thick puree. Season with kosher salt and freshly ground black pepper. Serve hot. Scatter diced tangerines on top.

Serves 6 (makes about 4 cups)

celery gratinée with prosciutto

Before doctors got into the act, celery was used as folk medicine to reduce inflammation from arthritis. In fact, it is mostly water and fiber, and by eating raw celery, it is jokingly said, you burn more calories chewing and digesting it than you consume. The cheese and prosciutto in this dish add protein and, of course, bold flavor.

1 large leafy bunch **celery**

½ cup freshly grated **Parmigiano-Reggiano**

1½ ounces thinly sliced **prosciutto**

Preheat oven to 400°F.

Cut about 5 inches from top of celery bunch. Save leaves for later. (Reserve top of stalks for another use.)

Cut remaining celery lengthwise through the root into 4 wedges. Wash thoroughly, leaving root end intact.

Bring a large pot of salted water to a boil. Add celery wedges and boil for 20 minutes. Drain immediately under cold water. Pat dry.

Place celery on a baking sheet, cut side up, with celery ribs slightly separated. Sprinkle with cheese. Bake for 10 minutes. Place under broiler until golden.

Remove from oven. Carefully transfer celery to a platter. Drape prosciutto over warm celery. Add a grinding of black pepper.

Serves 4

cipolle al forno

Get to know your onions: in the Middle Ages, they were believed to be so life-sustaining that onions were prized as wedding presents! These slow-roasted alliums anointed with olive oil help keep the blood thin and cholesterol down.

4 very large round **onions**: 2 yellow and 2 red

3 tablespoons **extra-virgin olive oil**

3 tablespoons **balsamic vinegar**

Preheat oven to 400°F.

Peel the onions, leaving 1 thin layer of skin. Cut them in half through the equator. Place cut side down in a heavy shallow roasting pan. Pour 2 tablespoons oil over the onions. Add a sprinkling of kosher salt and freshly ground black pepper.

Bake for 20 minutes. Cut side of onions will be black. Turn over and press down firmly with a spatula. Bake for another 15 minutes. Turn again, press again with a spatula, and bake for 20 minutes longer.

Remove onions from pan. Add the remaining oil and vinegar to the pan, and scrape up the browned bits. Pour pan juices over onions. Serve warm or at room temperature.

Serves 8

steamed cauliflower, garlicky breadcrumbs

Despite its wonderful flavor, this old-fashioned dish has fallen out of style—which is too bad because it has newly valued benefits: Eating cauliflower, and other cruciferous vegetables, is associated with low cancer rates in humans. One serving is also a credible source of vitamin C.

1 large head **cauliflower**

2½-ounce piece crusty **sourdough baguette**

2 tablespoons **garlic olive oil** (page 14) or store-bought

You can leave the cauliflower whole or cut it into large florets.

Wash cauliflower thoroughly, removing any dark spots with a small knife. I like to use the leafy green parts as well. Place whole cauliflower or florets in a steamer basket over boiling water. Cover tightly and steam florets for 15 to 18 minutes, whole cauliflower for 20 minutes, or until tender.

Meanwhile, cut bread into chunks and place in a food processor. Process until you have coarse crumbs, about ¾ cup. Add a pinch of kosher salt and freshly ground black pepper and mix.

Heat 1½ tablespoons garlic olive oil in a small nonstick skillet. Add crumbs and toast over medium heat, stirring constantly, until breadcrumbs are coated with oil and are crisp.

When ready to serve, place hot cauliflower on a platter. Drizzle with remaining ½ tablespoon garlic olive oil. Cover with breadcrumbs.

Serves 4

red chard with garlic cream

The history of chard dates back to the famous hanging gardens of ancient Babylonia. Developed from a wild strain of Mediterranean beets, red chard provides beta-carotene, vitamin C, iron, and a pleasantly bitter flavor. Sour cream adds a calcium boost. This is a great-looking dish but be forewarned—it is decidedly pink.

½ small clove **garlic,** peeled

⅓ cup low-fat **sour cream**

2 pounds red **Swiss chard**

Push garlic through a garlic press, and combine with sour cream in a small bowl. Season with kosher salt and freshly ground black pepper. Stir and set aside at room temperature.

Wash chard thoroughly and pat dry. Cut leaves into 1-inch pieces and stems into ½-inch pieces, then put in a pot with ½ cup water. Sprinkle lightly with salt. Cook, covered, over medium-high heat for 15 minutes, or until soft. Drain thoroughly in a colander and place in a bowl. Toss with garlic cream.

Add salt and coarsely ground black pepper to taste. Serve immediately.

Serves 4

five-minute corn with aged tamari

Corn has a seven-thousand-year history as both food and medicine. Rich in complex carbohydrates, it is a partial source of protein and is best eaten with beans, nuts, or dairy products. Tamari, a naturally fermented soy sauce without additives or preservatives (and usually without wheat), adds a taste more interesting than salt.

6 ears of **corn** in tightly closed husks

¼ cup Japanese aged **tamari**

¼ cup unsalted whipped **butter**

Wash husks without peeling corn. Bring a large pot of water to a boil. Add corn. Return to a boil and cook for 5 minutes.

Transfer corn to a platter. Let cool for 2 minutes and remove husks and silk. Discard silk.

Place husks on a platter. Top with cooked corn on the cob. Sprinkle tamari over corn and dot with butter. Dust with plenty of freshly ground black pepper. Serve more tamari at the table.

Serves 6

raspberry-kissed red cabbage

low calorie & fat-free

Red and green cabbages are both high in fiber, but red's ahead in vitamin C. To fix its color, red cabbage needs to be cooked with acid, which is why you see it in so many sweet-and-sour recipes. In this dish I've used raspberry vinegar for its aroma, and softened all the flavors by slowly braising the cabbage with aromatic honey.

1 medium **red cabbage**, about 2 pounds

⅓ cup **raspberry vinegar**

5 tablespoons best-quality **honey**: wild thyme, wildflower, or leatherwood

Remove core and any dark outer leaves from cabbage. Cut into ¼-inch-thick slices. Then cut these slices into ¼-inch squares.

Put cabbage in a large nonreactive pot. Add 3 cups water, vinegar, 3 tablespoons honey, 2 teaspoons kosher salt, and freshly ground black pepper. Stir.

Bring to a boil. Lower heat to maintain a simmer and cover pot. Cook for 2½ hours.

With a slotted spoon, transfer cabbage to a bowl. Add 2 tablespoons honey to liquid in pan and bring to a boil. Lower heat to medium and cook until liquid becomes thick and syrupy, and is reduced to about ½ cup. Pour over cabbage. Stir well. Add salt and pepper to taste. Serve hot or very cold. You can splash with additional raspberry vinegar, if desired.

Serves 6

baked quince in aromatics

low calorie & fat-free

In the spirit of full disclosure, I confess I'd never dealt with a quince until I began work on this book. Related to apples and pears, this fruit is inedible when raw and a revelation when cooked. It undergoes a wondrous transformation of color and texture, turning into a golden-red "sweetmeat"—the perfect accompaniment to poultry or pork. With a piece of mild cheese, it also makes a terrific dessert.

3 large firm **quinces**

6 tablespoons **sugar**

1½ tablespoons **pickling spice**

Preheat oven to 325°F.

Wash quinces and cut in half through the stem end. Core each half with a melon baller to remove seeds.

Place cut side down in a shallow ovenproof casserole with a cover. In a small bowl, mix sugar and 2½ cups water until sugar dissolves. Add pickling spice and a pinch of kosher salt. Stir and pour over quinces.

Cover and bake for 1 hour. Turn quinces over. Cover again and bake for 1 hour, then uncover, turn over, and bake for ½ hour. Turn again and bake for ½ hour longer if needed. Quinces should be very tender but retain their shape. Total baking time will be 2½ to 3 hours.

Using a slotted spoon, transfer quinces to a shallow bowl. Strain liquid into a small saucepan and cook liquid over medium-high heat for 8 to 10 minutes, until syrupy. Drizzle over slightly cooled quinces. Serve warm, at room temperature, or cold.

Serves 6

green vegetables à la vapeur

Here's health in a basket as three verdant vegetables are steamed together. One is turned into a buttery-tasting sauce that binds the flavors together. This trio, delicious hot or cold, is extremely low in calories.

¾ pound fresh **snow peas**

¾ pound fresh **green beans**

3 medium **zucchini**, about 1 pound

Remove tails from snow peas. Trim ends of green beans. Using a small sharp knife, cut beans in half lengthwise. Wash snow peas and beans in a colander and drain thoroughly.

Wash zucchini and pat dry. Cut 2 zucchini into ⅓-inch cubes.

Cut remaining 1 zucchini into 1-inch pieces and place in a small saucepan. Cover with water and add ¼ teaspoon salt. Bring to a boil. Lower heat and cook for 15 minutes, until zucchini is very soft.

Using a slotted spoon, transfer cooked zucchini to bowl of a food processor, reserving cooking water. Process until very smooth and creamy, adding almost all the cooking water. The sauce will be thick. You will have about ⅔ cup.

Bring large pot of water fitted with steamer basket to a boil. Place snow peas and green beans in basket. Place zucchini cubes on top. Cover and steam for 7 minutes.

Lightly salt vegetables and transfer to a serving platter. Cover with zucchini sauce. Add freshly ground black pepper to taste. Serve immediately. (This is also delicious cold.)

Serves 6

poached leeks with roasted garlic and brie fondue

Slender and graceful, leeks become silky when poached, and lose some of their edgy pungency. Garlic loses its edge when roasted and adds deep, mellow flavor to a sauce of creamy brie.

1 large head **garlic**

8 medium **leeks**, about 2 pounds

5 ounces **Brie** (4 ounces edible portion), well chilled

Preheat oven to 400°F.

Wrap garlic in a large piece of foil to make a pouch, and seal top tightly. Place in a pie tin and roast for 1 hour. Remove from oven, open foil packet, and let cool.

Trim leeks so that you have only 2 to 3 inches of dark green tops. Remove roots. Split in half lengthwise, stopping ½ inch from the root end, keeping leeks intact. Wash thoroughly between the leaves.

Fill a large skillet with enough water to cover leeks, about 2 inches. Add 1 tablespoon kosher salt and bring to a boil. Add leeks and lower heat to medium. Cover skillet and cook for 15 minutes, until soft.

Meanwhile, remove rind from cheese. Cut cheese into small pieces and place in a small saucepan. Add 2 tablespoons poaching liquid from the leeks. Cut cooked garlic in half through the diameter and squeeze out 1 heaping tablespoon garlic pulp. Reserve remaining garlic for another use. Add a pinch of freshly ground white pepper and heat, stirring constantly, until cheese melts.

Remove leeks from water and drain. Pour melted cheese over leeks. Serve immediately.

Serves 4

confit of carrots and lemon

Raw-vegetable enthusiasts should keep in mind that carotenes are better absorbed when cooked. You can substitute bunches of fresh baby carrots (but not those often tasteless plastic-bagged nubbins), or cut larger carrots into a variety of interesting shapes. I've also made this with red-tinged carrots, new on the market.

1¼ pounds medium-large organic **carrots** (weighed after removing carrot tops)

1 large **lemon**

2 tablespoons **extra-virgin olive oil**

Peel carrots. Cut the carrots on the bias into ¼-inch-thick, long oval slices.

Place carrots in a 4-quart saucepan. Cut lemon in half. Slice one half into thin rounds and add to pot. Squeeze the other half and add juice to pot with the oil, ¼ cup water, ¼ teaspoon kosher salt, and 6 black peppercorns.

Bring to a boil. Cover pot and lower heat to maintain a simmer. Cook for 35 to 40 minutes. Do not lift the lid. Shake pot back and forth several times during cooking.

Uncover and stir. Add kosher salt and pepper to taste, if desired. Garnish serving platter with sprigs of lacy carrot tops.

Serves 4

oven-roasted peppers, za'atar oil

For me there are few spices as evocative as za'atar, which strongly summons my days of wandering the old city of Jerusalem. Khaki-hued, za'atar is a mixture of hyssop, ground sumac, and sesame seeds. It is earthy and addictive, with a curious Mediterranean air. Nutritionists make no health claims for za'atar, but I know what it does for the soul.

8 very large **red bell peppers**

4½ tablespoons **extra-virgin olive oil**

2 tablespoons **za'atar** (see Note), plus more for garnish

Preheat oven to 375°F.

Wash peppers. Cut in half lengthwise. Remove core and seeds.

Place cut side down in a large shallow roasting pan. Spoon 3 tablespoons oil over top. Sprinkle with kosher salt and freshly ground black pepper. Roast for 50 minutes, until skins are browned.

Remove from oven. Transfer peppers to a platter. Collect all pan juices and put in a small bowl, adding a little water to the pan and scraping up browned bits if necessary. Add remaining oil and za'atar to pan juices. Add salt if necessary.

Pour over peppers. Serve hot, warm, or at room temperature. Dust with additional za'atar, if desired.

Serves 8

Note: Za'atar is a spice blend available in Middle Eastern food stores. Use the green variety from Lebanon or Israel.

petite ratatouille

This stripped-down ratatouille delivers the welcome clarity of simple food lovingly cooked over slow heat, for their natural juices coax the vegetables into another dimension. The olives deliver heart-healthy compounds and, said author Lawrence Durrell, "a taste older than wine; a taste as old as cold water." Try this dish both warm and cold for two quite different taste sensations.

3 medium **zucchini,** about 1¼ pounds

12 ounces small **cherry tomatoes**: use a mixture of red and yellow if possible

16 **kalamata olives**, about 3 ounces

Preheat oven to 300°F.

Wash zucchini and trim ends. Cut in half lengthwise. Cut into ½-inch-thick half circles. Place in a large bowl.

Wash cherry tomatoes and cut in half. Add to bowl. Add olives, pitting them if you wish, and mix thoroughly.

Pour ¼ cup cold water over vegetables. Add a large pinch of sea salt and freshly ground black pepper. Mix again.

Place in a shallow 9-by-11-inch casserole. Bake for 2 hours, stirring every 30 minutes.

Transfer, with any juices, to a serving bowl. Add salt and pepper to taste. Let cool. Serve at room temperature or serve cold.

Serves 4

apples and cranberries: relish and compote

Before apples were keeping doctors away in America, cranberries were doing the job, for they were used by indigenous people as both food and medicine. They provide fiber and vitamin C. These two recipes demonstrate how differently the same ingredients taste when raw and when cooked.

RELISH

4 medium Macintosh **apples**, about 1¼ pounds

½ cup raw **cranberries**

¼ cup **light brown sugar**

Peel apples and cut into ½-inch pieces, removing cores and seeds. Place in bowl of a food processor with cranberries, sugar, and a pinch of kosher salt. Process until it is the texture of a smooth salsa with tiny discernable pieces. You do not want a puree but a relish with some texture. Refrigerate until cold.

Serves 4

COMPOTE

4 medium Macintosh **apples**, about 1¼ pounds

1 scant cup raw **cranberries**

5 tablespoons **light brown sugar**

Peel apples and cut into ½-inch pieces, removing cores and seeds. Place in a 4-quart saucepan with cranberries, sugar, and 1 cup water. Bring to a boil. Cover pot and cook over moderate heat for about 20 minutes, stirring occasionally. Remove from heat and stir vigorously with a wooden spoon until apples and cranberries are broken down and sauce is fairly smooth. Let cool, then refrigerate until cold.

Serves 4

carrot puree in roasted onion cups

Although this robust recipe stands up to strong-flavored meats as a dramatic side dish, it also makes a stunning main course set in a bed of contrasting grains such as buckwheat groats or coarse bulghur wheat.

7 large **onions** (about ½ pound each)

2 tablespoons **olive oil**

1½ pounds slender **carrots**

Preheat oven to 425°F.

Peel and finely dice 1 onion. Set aside. Cut roots from remaining onions, but do not peel. Cut a small slice from root ends so that onions sit upright. Cut ¾-inch-thick "hats" from tops of onions. Using your hands, coat each onion with a little olive oil, using up to ½ tablespoon, and place root end up on a baking sheet. Bake for 1 to 1½ hours until soft.

Meanwhile, peel carrots and slice into ⅛-inch-thick coins. Heat remaining 1½ tablespoons oil in a large nonstick skillet and add diced onions. Cook over medium heat for 5 minutes, or until soft but not brown. Add carrots and raise heat to medium. Add ½ teaspoon kosher salt and freshly ground black pepper. Cook carrots and onions, stirring often, until soft and golden, about 20 minutes. Add ½ cup water and cook over high heat for 2 minutes, until water is absorbed. Add another ½ cup water and cook over high heat for 2 minutes longer. Some water will remain. Transfer to a food processor and process just until smooth. You will have 2 cups of puree.

When onions are soft, remove from oven. When cool enough to handle, remove outer skins and, using a small knife, scoop out about a third from the center of each onion. Discard or save for another use. Fill with carrot puree and place under broiler until lightly browned. Serve immediately.

Serves 6

julienned snow peas with lemon oil and poppy seeds

low calorie & low fat

When julienned and steamed, snow peas retain their beautiful verdance and subtle crunch. Poppy seeds add drama—and a taste that's hard to describe.

1¼ pounds **snow peas**

2 tablespoons plus 1 teaspoon **lemon olive oil** (page 14, and see Note)

1½ teaspoons **poppy seeds**, plus more for garnish

Wash snow peas. Remove tips, tails, and fibrous strings. Using a sharp knife, cut each snow pea lengthwise into 4 or 5 julienned strips.

Bring a pot of water to a boil. Fit with a steamer basket. Place julienned snow peas in steamer. Cover tightly and steam over boiling water for 7 to 8 minutes until just tender, but still crunchy.

Transfer cooked snow peas to a bowl. Add lemon olive oil, poppy seeds, kosher salt to taste, and a generous grinding of black pepper. Toss well. Sprinkle with additional poppy seeds if desired and serve immediately.
Serves 6

Note: Lemon-flavored olive oils from Boyajian or Land of Canaan (Israel) are available in many supermarkets and specialty food stores, and are kosher.

steamed mustard greens, roasted garlic butter

low calorie

The combination of bitter greens and sweet roasted garlic is one of the most delicious vegetable preparations I know. Turnip greens make an equally beneficial substitute and are abundant in absorbable calcium.

1 large head **garlic**

1½ pounds **mustard greens** or collard greens

3 tablespoons unsalted whipped **butter**

Preheat oven to 400°F.

Wrap garlic head in a large piece of foil to make a pouch, and seal top tightly. Place in a pie tin and roast for 1 hour. Remove from oven, open foil packet, and let cool.

Wash greens thoroughly and pat dry.

Cut garlic in half through the equator. Squeeze 2 tablespoons pulp from garlic. Place butter in a small bowl and, using a fork, mash garlic pulp into butter, mixing well.

In a large nonstick skillet or a shallow flame-proof casserole large enough to hold all the greens, heat half the butter mixture. Add greens and cook over high heat until wilted. Add remaining butter mixture, and kosher salt and freshly ground black pepper to taste. Stirring constantly, continue to cook for 5 to 8 minutes, over medium heat, until tender. Serve immediately.
Serves 4

summer squash with fresh basil

For a change of pace, try grating summer squash instead of slicing them into the familiar rounds. The new texture is interesting, and faster cooking preserves its nutrients.

1¾ pounds small yellow **squash**

1 large bunch **basil**

1½ tablespoons plus 1 teaspoon unsalted **butter**

Wash squash and trim ends. Grate on large holes of box grater. Place in a bowl.

Wash basil and dry thoroughly. Chop enough basil leaves to yield ⅔ cup, reserving remaining leaves for garnish. Add chopped basil to bowl with ¼ teaspoon sea salt and freshly ground black pepper to taste. Stir.

In a large nonstick skillet, melt butter. Add squash mixture and cook over medium heat for 10 minutes, stirring often. Do not let squash brown. Cook until squash is soft. Add additional salt and pepper if necessary. Serve hot.

Garnish with small basil leaves.

Serves 4

vibrant spinach-fennel puree

Spinach is a good example of why it's important to eat those leafy greens: It is endowed with beta-carotene, folic acid, magnesium, potassium, and iron. Fennel, while a nutritional lightweight, adds fiber, flavor, and those feathery fronds for garnish.

2 large bunches curly **spinach**, about 1½ pounds

1 large **fennel** bulb, about 1 pound

2 tablespoons plus 1 teaspoon unsalted **butter**

Wash spinach thoroughly. Remove thick stems and discard. Set leaves aside.

Remove feathery fronds from fennel and reserve for garnish. Remove and discard core. Cut fennel into ½-inch pieces. Place in a pot (large enough to accommodate the spinach) with enough water to cover. Bring to a boil. Lower heat to medium and cook, covered, for 20 minutes, until very soft.

Add spinach to pot, and bring to a boil. Cook for 2 to 3 minutes, until spinach is tender but still bright green.

Immediately drain fennel and spinach in a colander under cold running water to fix color. Drain thoroughly. Place in bowl of a food processor. Cut butter into small pieces and add to processor. Process until very smooth.

Transfer to saucepan. Add freshly ground black pepper to taste. Heat gently before serving. Garnish with finely chopped fennel fronds and coarse sea salt.

Serves 4

tomatoes arrosti on a bed of thyme

This is a wonderful end-of-summer recipe—or, a good technique to maximize tomatoes' flavor at other times of the year. The lycopene in red tomatoes is said to protect against prostate cancer and is more readily available to the body when cooked with olive oil. The essential oils in fresh thyme invigorate the lungs and quiet stomach cramps, herbalists say. The ancient Greeks used thyme as medicine and considered it a symbol of bravery.

10 red **tomatoes**: a mixure of plum, whole large red on the vine, and small beefsteak, about 3 pounds

2 large bunches fresh **thyme**

2 tablespoons plus 1 teaspoon **extra-virgin olive oil**

Preheat oven to 275°F.

Wash tomatoes. Cut plum tomatoes in half through the stem end. Cut other varieties horizontally.

On a large rimmed baking sheet, place a layer of thyme. Place tomatoes, cut side down, on top. Cover with another layer of thyme, saving some for later use. Drizzle with olive oil. Sprinkle lightly with sea salt and freshly ground black pepper.

Roast for 2 hours. Carefully turn tomatoes over and bake 1 hour longer. Remove from oven. Remove top layer of thyme. Place the top layer of crisp thyme branches on a large platter and with a spatula transfer tomatoes to the platter, placing cut side down over the thyme.

Sprinkle with fresh thyme leaves. Serve warm or at room temperature.

Serves 4

rosemary-roasted turnips

Purple and white, turnips are robust root vegetables high in fiber and vitamin C. Slow roasting mellows their bite by intensifying natural sugars. Once upon a time, rosemary was purported to be a strong memory stimulant; ancient Greeks wore sprigs in their hair to remind them to go home for dinner.

6 medium-large **turnips**, about 2 pounds

1 small bunch **rosemary**

2½ tablespoons **extra-virgin olive oil**

Preheat oven to 375°F.

Peel the turnips and cut each into 6 to 8 wedges.

Finely chop 3 tablespoons rosemary needles. Using a mortar and pestle, make a paste of the rosemary, 2 tablespoons olive oil, and 1½ teaspoons kosher salt. (You can also use a blender.)

Place rosemary mixture in a bowl and add the turnips. Toss to coat, adding ½ tablespoon oil.

Season with a grinding of black pepper.

Place in a shallow roasting pan or on a baking sheet. Bake for 40 to 45 minutes, frequently turning over turnips so each side gets browned. Cook until golden brown and tender.

Remove from oven and transfer to a platter. Sprinkle with additional finely chopped rosemary. Serve hot.

Serves 6

yucca puree with buttermilk and chives

low calorie & low fat

No one will guess what this is, but everyone will love it. Also known as manioc or cassava, yucca is a dark brown tuber with a barklike rind protecting a pure white interior; you pass it often in your supermarket's Latino vegetable section. Always eaten cooked, it's a hip alternative to mashed potatoes. Buttermilk gives this starchy tuber an ultra-creamy mouth feel, and protein and calcium.

1 large **yucca**, about 1¼ pounds

¾ cup low-fat **buttermilk**

1 bunch **chives**

Cut yucca across the width into 4 pieces. Using a small sharp knife, carefully cut away waxy brown rind, leaving only the white flesh.

Bring a pot of heavily salted water to a boil. Add yucca and cook over high heat for 20 to 25 minutes, until very tender but not falling apart.

Using a slotted spoon, transfer yucca to bowl of a food processor. Process, gradually adding all but 2 tablespoons buttermilk, until very smooth and thick.

Transfer to a serving bowl. Add kosher salt and freshly ground black pepper to taste. Finely mince 3 tablespoons chives. Drizzle 2 tablespoons buttermilk over puree and strew with chives. Serve immediately.

Serves 4

wild mushrooms in marsala

low calorie

Splurge on the best mushrooms you can find. Varieties abound: porcini, oyster mushrooms, black trumpets, morels, chanterelles, hen-of-the-woods, and shiitakes, to name a few. Shiitakes in particular contain elements that stimulate the immune system; they are used in Eastern medicine to prevent high blood pressure and heart disease, and to reduce cholesterol. They also have a strong, lingering perfume.

14 ounces mixed **wild mushrooms**

⅓ cup **heavy cream**

5 tablespoons **Marsala**

Wipe mushrooms with a damp cloth. Remove bottom half of stems. Cut mushrooms in half.

In a 10-inch nonstick skillet, heat heavy cream. Cook over high heat until it starts to thicken and bubble, about 1 minute. Add 2 tablespoons Marsala and the mushrooms.

Add ¼ teaspoon fine sea salt, and stirring constantly, cook over medium heat until mushrooms begin to soften, about 3 minutes.

Add remaining Marsala and lots of freshly ground black pepper to taste.

Cook over high heat for 2 minutes longer, until mushrooms release most of their liquid. When the mushrooms are tender (but still retain their shape), remove from the pan using a slotted spoon and place on a platter. Continue to cook pan juices over high heat for 20 to 30 seconds, until juices thicken. Pour over mushrooms. Sprinkle with a little sea salt and more freshly ground pepper. Serve immediately.

Serves 4

lemon spinach with toasted pistachios

A touch of lemon-laced olive oil brightens the grassy flavor of spinach, and a quick sauté preserves the integrity of the leaves. A handful of pistachios adds some vitamins, minerals, and a little healthy fat. All in five minutes.

2 pounds curly **spinach**

1 ounce shelled **pistachio nuts**, about ¼ packed cup

1 tablespoon plus 1 teaspoon **lemon olive oil** (page 14, and see Note)

Remove stems from spinach and discard. Wash leaves thoroughly and pat dry.

In a small nonstick skillet, toast pistachios over medium heat until they begin to turn brown and their aroma rises. Transfer to a cutting board and chop coarsely. Set aside.

In a large nonstick skillet, heat lemon olive oil. When hot, add spinach and cook over high heat until it wilts, stirring constantly. Add fine sea salt and freshly ground black pepper to taste.

Scatter nuts over spinach. Serve immediately.
Serves 4

Note: Lemon-flavored olive oils from Boyajian or Land of Canaan (Israel) are available in many supermarkets and specialty food stores, and are kosher.

baked potatoes with truffle oil and thyme

low calorie

There's a culinary irony about pouring precious truffle oil over a humble baked potato. Exalted to celebrity status by New York's Four Seasons restaurant (which charges twenty dollars for the luxury spud), it is an inspired dish. Since most of a potato's nutrients are in or near the skin, I suggest you buy organic, then eat it all and breathe in deeply.

4 small organic **baking potatoes**

2 tablespoons **truffle oil**

1 bunch fresh **thyme**

Preheat oven to 400°F.

Scrub potatoes thoroughly. Prick in several places with a fork. Sprinkle skin lightly with salt. Place directly on oven rack and bake for 1 hour.

Cut a ½-inch oval slice from top of each baked potato.

Using a fork, fluff up inside of potato. Pour ½ tablespoon truffle oil into each potato. Sprinkle with sea salt, freshly ground black pepper, and 1 teaspoon thyme leaves.

Place potato on a small bed of thyme branches or on a bed of coarse sea salt heated in the oven. Serve immediately.

Serves 4

garlic-mashed yukon golds

low calorie

"True food for the heart," says my clinical herbalist of garlic (she eats at least two cloves a day). This natural antibiotic-in-plant-form stimulates immune functions and lowers blood cholesterol. Potatoes are rich in potassium; extra-virgin olive oil is rich in protective phytochemicals.

2 pounds **Yukon gold potatoes**

12 large cloves **garlic**

¼ cup **extra-virgin olive oil**

Peel potatoes and garlic. Put potatoes and 10 cloves garlic in a 4-quart pot. Add cold water to cover potatoes. Add 1 teaspoon kosher salt and bring to a boil. Lower heat to medium-high and cover, leaving the lid askew. Cook until tender, about 35 minutes.

Meanwhile, heat 1 tablespoon oil in a small nonstick skillet. Slice remaining garlic paper-thin and add to skillet. Cook over low heat until very soft but not brown, about 5 minutes. Set aside.

When potatoes are cooked, drain in a colander, reserving 1¼ cups cooking water. Push potatoes and garlic through a ricer, or place in a large bowl and, using a potato masher, mash thoroughly. Add 3 tablespoons remaining oil and cooked sliced garlic in its oil, and gradually add enough cooking water, mixing constantly, to make a smooth creamy consistency. Add salt and freshly ground white pepper to taste. Serve hot.

Serves 8

scalloped cheese potatoes

Sounds too good to be good for you? Three simple ingredients add up to a low-cal and low-fat side dish, full of flavor and nutrients. Potatoes supply B vitamins, potassium, and easily digestible starch for energy. Asiago, a sturdy cow's milk cheese from northern Italy, provides calcium and great taste.

4 large Idaho **potatoes**, about 2 pounds

2¾ ounces **Asiago cheese**, grated

2 cups fat-free **chicken broth**

Preheat oven to 375°F.

Cut a round of parchment paper to fit the bottom of an 8½-inch springform pan.

Peel potatoes and slice into paper-thin rounds.

Sprinkle 2 tablespoons grated cheese onto paper in pan. Top with one-quarter of the potatoes, placed in one layer with slices overlapping. Sprinkle with 2 tablespoons cheese, and freshly ground black pepper to taste.

Repeat 3 more times. You will have 4 layers of potatoes. Before adding last layer of cheese, pour chicken broth over potatoes. Press down with spatula. Sprinkle with remaining grated cheese.

Place pan on a baking sheet. Bake for 1 hour 20 minutes. Potatoes will be tender and will have absorbed the broth. Cheese will be golden brown.

Remove from springform, cut into wedges, and serve immediately.

Serves 6

snow peas in the french style

Snow peas, once considered a cliché of Cantonese restaurants in America, became the darlings of nouvelle cuisine. They are called *mange-tout* in French, which means "eat the whole thing." This classic sauté with shallots and butter is an utterly French preparation.

1 pound **snow peas**

5 large **shallots**, about 6 ounces

1 tablespoon plus 2 teaspoons unsalted **butter**

Wash snow peas and pat dry. Remove tips, tails, and fibrous strings.

Place in a steamer basket over boiling water. Cover tightly and steam for 2 minutes. Place in a colander under cold running water. Pat dry.

Peel shallots and chop finely. In a large non-stick skillet, melt butter and add shallots. Cook, stirring, over medium heat for several minutes, until shallots soften and become translucent. You do not want them to brown. Add snow peas and cook for 3 minutes, until tender and hot. Do not overcook; you want the snow peas to remain bright green. Season with coarse sea salt (*sel gris* is best) and freshly ground black pepper. Serve immediately.

Serves 4

crispy cumin potatoes

Our friend Suvir Saran, culinary scholar and caterer extraordinaire, hails from New Delhi, where this delicious potato dish was a favorite in his grandmother's house. Grapeseed oil withstands the high temperatures needed for supernal crispness. Cumin seed, cultivated in the Nile Valley five thousand years ago, is considered an essential spice by those in the know. It adds intriguing flavor and is said to promote assimilation of starchy vegetables.

3 large waxy **potatoes**: Yukon gold or red bliss, about 8 ounces each

3 tablespoons **grapeseed oil**

2 teaspoons **cumin seed**

Scrub potatoes but do not peel. Place in a pot with enough salted water to cover. Bring to a boil. Lower heat to medium, cover pot, and cook until tender, about 30 minutes. Drain potatoes. Let cool and refrigerate until very cold.

Peel potatoes and cut into 1-inch chunks.

Heat oil in a large nonstick skillet. Add cumin seed and cook for 30 seconds. Add potatoes and cook over medium-high heat for 10 to 15 minutes, turning often so that all sides get crisp.

Sprinkle with fine sea salt and freshly ground black pepper. Serve immediately.

Serves 5 to 6

my favorite sweet potatoes

The alpha- and beta-carotenes in sweet potatoes are thought to deter many ailments due to oxidative damage. These tubers are also a great source of energy. My experience with this recipe is that absolutely no one will believe there's no butter, cream, or any other fat lurking in the background.

4 large **sweet potatoes**, about 3 pounds

2 juice **oranges**

2-inch piece fresh **ginger**

Scrub potatoes, but do not peel. Place in a pot with enough cold water to cover. Bring to a boil, then lower heat to medium. Cook for 50 minutes, or until potatoes are very soft.

Meanwhile, grate rind of 1 orange on fine holes of box grater to yield 1 teaspoon grated zest. Cut oranges in half and squeeze ⅔ cup juice. Set aside.

Drain potatoes in colander and peel thoroughly under cool running water. Cut into large chunks and place in bowl of a food processor.

Using a small sharp knife, peel ginger and mince. You should have almost ¼ cup.

Add orange zest, juice, and ginger to food processor with potatoes. Process until very smooth. Transfer mixture to a saucepan and add kosher salt to taste. Do not add pepper, as the ginger provides enough heat. Reheat gently before serving.

Serves 8

two-in-one string bean and red onion puree: hot vegetable and cold dip

String beans are harvested young, when both pods and seeds are tender. They provide beta-carotene, calcium, potassium, and crunch, which says a lot about a skinny vegetable. This is a lovely hot side dish which can double as a cold dip served with crudités or parmesan crisps (page 33).

2 large red **onions**, about 1 pound

2 tablespoons **walnut oil**

1½ pounds **string beans**, preferably green

Peel onions and cut into ¼-inch dice. Heat 1½ tablespoons walnut oil in a large nonstick skillet. Add onions, a pinch of kosher salt, and freshly ground black pepper, and cook over high heat for 5 minutes, stirring often. Lower heat to medium and cook for about 25 minutes, stirring occasionally, until onions are dark brown and soft.

Meanwhile, wash beans and trim ends. Cut beans into 1-inch pieces. Bring a large pot of salted water to a boil. Add beans, bring back to a rapid boil, and continue to boil for 15 minutes. Drain in a colander under cold water. Pat dry.

Toss beans with caramelized onions, scraping up any browned bits in the skillet. Place in bowl of food processor and process until almost smooth but still a bit gravel-like in texture. Add remaining ½ tablespoon walnut oil, and salt and pepper to taste. Return puree to skillet and cook over medium-high heat until hot. Serve as a side dish. Alternately, chill until very cold and serve as a dip for crudités, on a leaf of lettuce, or as a filling for cherry tomatoes.

Serves 6 (makes about 3½ cups)

tiny lentils with port-glazed shallots

Botanically speaking, beans, peas, and lentils are related—the seeds of vegetables that have pods and are, as a group, known as pulses or legumes. This dish is especially rich in flavor and health attributes: port provides the same benefits as other red wines; lentils supply B vitamins, iron, and folic acid.

1½ cups ruby **port**

½ pound small shallots plus 3 large **shallots**

1 pound tiny green French **lentils**, about 2 cups

Place port in a medium saucepan. Peel ½ pound shallots. Add to saucepan. Bring to a slow simmer and cook, uncovered, for 50 minutes, stirring occasionally. The port will reduce substantially and glaze the shallots. The shallots will retain their shape but be tender when pierced with the tip of a sharp knife. Set aside.

Meanwhile, put lentils in a medium-large saucepan. Peel remaining shallots and finely mince. You will have about 3 tablespoons minced shallots. Add to lentils with ½ teaspoon whole black peppercorns and 1 teaspoon kosher salt. Cover with 8 cups cold water. Bring to a boil. Lower heat, cover pot, and simmer for 35 to 40 minutes, until tender but not mushy.

Drain lentils and put in a serving bowl.

When ready to serve, reheat glazed shallots and pour shallots and reduced port over the hot lentils; stir gently. Season with salt and freshly ground black pepper.

Serves 8

sugar snaps and sweet pepper julienne, red pepper sauce

low calorie

My nutritionist says that the more colorful the food the greater the benefit—and this dish is an excellent example. Bright green sugar snap peas and strips of vibrant red pepper are awash in a sauce of peppers pureed in roasted peanut oil. A fairly new vegetable in markets, sugar snaps resemble peas-in-the-pod, but their pods are shorter, plumper, darker, and you can eat the pod and the peas inside.

1 pound **sugar snap peas**

2 medium-large **red bell peppers**

3 tablespoons **roasted peanut oil** (see Note)

Remove ends of pods and their fibrous strings. This is important.

Bring a pot of salted water to a boil. Add peas and boil for 3 minutes, until just beginning to soften. They should be bright green. Drain in a colander and refresh under cold running water.

Cut peppers in half lengthwise. Remove core and seeds. Cut 3 halves into long, thin julienne strips.

Cut remaining half pepper into ½-inch squares. Place in a blender with 1 tablespoon peanut oil, 1 tablespoon water, and a pinch of kosher salt and freshly ground black pepper. Process for several minutes, until very smooth.

Heat remaining 2 tablespoons peanut oil in a nonstick skillet. Add julienned peppers and cook over medium heat for 2 minutes, until they begin to soften. Add sugar snaps and continue to cook until tender. Do not overcook. Add red pepper sauce. Heat briefly, adding salt and pepper to taste. Serve hot, warm, or at room temperature. *Serves 6*

Note: Roasted peanut oil is available in many supermarkets, specialty food stores, and health food shops.

big white beans in pesto

Look for the largest white beans (such as gigantes) you can find or, in a pinch, use cannellini (also known as white kidney beans). *Health* magazine dubbed beans one of their "top ten anticancer foods"—so make this dish often and qualify as a *mangiafagioli,* which means "bean-eater" in Tuscany, whence this dish originates.

12 ounces dried **large white beans**

5 large cloves **garlic**

4 tablespoons **pesto,** homemade or store-bought

Soak beans overnight in enough cold water to cover by 2 inches. Alternatively, place beans in a pot with water to cover; boil for 2 minutes and let sit, off heat, for 1 hour.

Drain beans and rinse in a colander. Place in a large pot with cold water to cover by 2 inches. Add 1 tablespoon kosher salt and ½ teaspoon whole black peppercorns.

Peel garlic. Chop all but ½ clove very finely. Add to beans. Bring to a boil and boil for 2 minutes. Lower heat to maintain a simmer. Cover pot and cook for 1 hour 45 minutes, or until beans are quite tender but still retain their shape. Drain beans in a colander, reserving 2 cups cooking liquid. Place beans and half of reserved cooking liquid in a bowl. Push remaining ½ clove garlic through a garlic press, and add it to beans; add pesto, salt and pepper to taste, and additional cooking liquid if necessary. Heat gently in a saucepan before serving. Serve immediately.

Serves 10

bulghur with morels and dried cherries

Bulghur is wheat that's been steamed, dried, and cracked. "Fine" bulghur is used in tabbouleh; the coarser variety goes into pilafs such as this. Ancient Chinese doctors believed the woodsy morel was a tonic to the stomach and regulated *qi,* the flow of vital energy.

½ ounce **dried morel mushrooms**

½ cup **dried cherries**, about 2 ounces

1 cup coarse **bulghur wheat**

Put morels in a bowl. Bring 3 cups water to a boil, pour over mushrooms, and let sit for 20 minutes. Strain mushroom liquid through a fine-mesh sieve lined with rinsed cheesecloth.

In a 4-quart pot, bring mushroom soaking liquid, ½ teaspoon kosher salt, and freshly ground black pepper to a boil.

Coarsely chop mushrooms. Add to boiling broth along with three-quarters of cherries. Add bulghur and cook over medium heat for 20 minutes. Cover pot and cook for about 10 minutes, until all the liquid is absorbed and bulghur is tender. Remove cover and fluff bulghur with a fork.

Add salt and pepper to taste. Chop remaining cherries and mix into bulghur. Serve hot.

Serves 4

buckwheat groats with "caramelized" onions

Kasha is made from buckwheat groats, which are the seeds of the rhubarb-related buckwheat plant, and not, as is commonly believed, a grain. The groats are hulled, roasted, and cracked. Nutty and chewy, groats are high in protein and are a great source of complex carbohydrates. My new cooking technique eliminates the need for kasha's traditional egg and fat. "Caramelized" onions, also fat-free, are slowly burnished in soy-based teriyaki sauce. Sprinkle some uncooked toasted groats atop this dish for extra crunch.

1 large white **onion**, about ½ pound

5 tablespoons **teriyaki sauce**

2 cups toasted **buckwheat groats**, about 11 ounces

Peel onion and cut into ¼-inch dice. Place in a medium nonstick skillet. Add ½ cup cold water, 4 tablespoons teriyaki sauce, and freshly ground black pepper to taste. Stir well and pat down so that onions are in a single layer. Bring to a boil. Boil for 3 minutes, then lower heat to maintain a simmer. Simmer for 15 to 20 minutes, until very soft. Onions will look caramelized and most of the liquid will have evaporated.

Meanwhile, in a medium pot bring 6 cups water and 1 teaspoon salt to a rapid boil. Add groats and stir. Lower heat to maintain a simmer. Cover pot and cook for 10 minutes. After 10 minutes, groats should be tender, but not too soft. Drain immediately in a fine-mesh sieve. Transfer to a warm bowl. Add hot caramelized onions and any pan juices to groats. Add remaining tablespoon teriyaki sauce and fluff with a fork. Add kosher salt and pepper to taste.

Serves 8

minted couscous with curry oil

Thai-style curry oil, now available in supermarkets and Asian food stores, is a staple in my twenty-first-century pantry; it is a simple way to add complexity to many dishes. When mixed with slivers of fresh mint atop a steamy mound of couscous, its truly seductive aromas are released. Couscous, tiny balls of semolina pasta, provides carbohydrates for quick energy.

1 cup **couscous**

1 tablespoon plus 1 teaspoon **Thai curry oil**

1 small bunch **mint**

Put 1¾ cups water in a medium pot. Add 1 tablespoon curry oil and ½ teaspoon kosher salt and bring to a boil.

Slowly add couscous, stirring, and cook over high heat for 1 minute, until couscous begins to thicken. Lower heat and continue to cook for 1 minute.

Cover pot, remove from heat, and let sit for 5 minutes.

Meanwhile, julienne or finely chop enough mint to yield 4 tablespoons. Set aside.

Fluff couscous with a fork, breaking up any small clumps. Transfer to a bowl. Add chopped mint and remaining teaspoon curry oil, stirring with a fork. Add salt and freshly ground black pepper to taste.

Garnish with fresh mint sprigs. Serve hot.

Serves 4

little tomato-pesto "napoleons"

These intensely flavored layers of vegetables stack up a rainbow of benefits: antioxidant, antiviral, antimicrobial—but certainly not antigastronomadic (*gastronomadic* is a word invented by the French chef Carême to describe tourists who are lovers of regional food specialties). Bake these in custard cups and think of Provence. Delicious hot, cold, or in between.

8 ripe **tomatoes**: 4 medium red, 2 medium-large yellow, 2 medium-large green, about 3 pounds

2 medium **yellow onions**

6 tablespoons **pesto**, homemade or store-bought

Preheat oven to 325°F.

Wash tomatoes and dry thoroughly. Cut red tomatoes in half horizontally. Lightly coat 8 custard cups with nonstick vegetable spray and place tomatoes in them cut side up.

Peel onions and cut each into 12 thin slices. Top each tomato with 1 onion slice. Spread 1 teaspoon pesto over each onion slice.

Cut each yellow tomato into 4 thick slices. Place a slice on top of each pesto-smeared onion slice. Top with another onion slice. Spread 1 teaspoon pesto on top.

Cut each green tomato into 4 thick slices. Place on top of onion. Top with another thin slice of onion. Spread with ¼ teaspoon pesto.

Place custard cups on a rimmed baking sheet. Bake for 1½ hours, carefully pouring off liquid every 30 minutes, and pressing down on napoleons with a spatula. Collect all juices in a small bowl.

When finished, let napoleons cool for a few minutes. Place juices in a small nonstick skillet and cook over high heat until juices are syrupy—reduced to about ½ cup. Add kosher salt and freshly ground black pepper to taste. Turn napoleons out onto a platter. Pour reduced juices over top and serve.

Serves 8

polenta with gorgonzola and peas

Whether called mamaliga, polenta, or cornmeal mush, this is a premier comfort food. Made from coarsely ground corn kernels, polenta provides a complete protein when combined with legumes. Gorgonzola adds protein and, above all, incomparable flavor. Be sure to use an imported one from Italy.

½ cup small fresh or frozen **peas**

1 cup yellow stone-ground **cornmeal**

2 ounces **Gorgonzola**

Cook fresh peas in a small amount of salted water until just tender, about 15 minutes. If using frozen, cook for 2 minutes. Drain in a colander under cold running water. Pat dry.

In a 4-quart saucepan, bring 3 cups water and ½ teaspoon kosher salt to a boil. Gradually add cornmeal, whisking constantly. Lower heat and cook for 2 minutes, until polenta thickens. Add cheese and continue to cook for 1 minute, stirring constantly. Add freshly ground black pepper and peas. Cook for 30 seconds, stirring constantly.

Serve immediately; alternatively, spoon polenta into 4 custard cups or timbales that have been sprayed with nonstick vegetable spray or into a 4- or 5-cup soufflé dish. Set aside until ready to serve. Cover with foil and heat in a 350°F oven for 10 minutes. Place briefly under broiler until golden. Serve hot.

Serves 4

brown rice with currants and dill

Nutty brown rice has only its husk removed during milling, leaving its valuable bran coating intact. Rich in complex carbohydrates, brown rice contains soluble and insoluble fiber and B-group vitamins. In this recipe, currants are tiny dried grapes that add potassium and phosphorous and have nothing to do with seasonal fresh currants. Dill, used both in medicine and the kitchen since ancient times, adds grassy aromatics to this wholesome dish.

1 cup long-grain **brown rice**

⅓ cup **currants**

1 large bunch fresh **dill**

In a large saucepan, put rice, 2½ cups water, and scant ½ teaspoon kosher salt. Bring to a boil. Immediately lower heat to maintain a simmer and cover pot. Simmer for 40 minutes, until all water is absorbed and rice is tender.

Meanwhile, place currants in a small bowl and cover with boiling water. Let sit for 10 minutes to plump. Drain.

Wash dill and dry thoroughly. Chop finely to yield ½ packed cup.

When rice is cooked, transfer to a warm bowl. Add drained currants and chopped dill. Toss gently to combine. Add freshly ground black pepper to taste. Serve immediately.

Serves 4

persian rice with saffron broth

In this recipe, precious threads of golden saffron tint and flavor aromatic basmati rice, and "linen steaming" allows a highly desirable bottom crust to develop. The accompanying liquid fools the eye, for it looks like a vat of melted butter.

½ teaspoon **saffron threads**

1½ cups **basmati rice**

2½ tablespoons unsalted **butter**

Put 2 quarts water, saffron, and 1½ tablespoons kosher salt in a pot. Bring to a boil. Add rice and boil for 10 minutes. Drain rice in a colander, reserving the saffron cooking liquid.

Melt 2 tablespoons butter in a 3- or 4-quart pot with a tight-fitting cover. Add rice and cover pot with a clean kitchen towel, then fit the lid over the towel. Fold edges of towel up over lid. Cook over low heat for 35 to 40 minutes so that a crust forms on the bottom.

Meanwhile, bring reserved saffron liquid to a boil and cook over medium heat for 5 minutes. Add ½ tablespoon butter and freshly ground white pepper to taste. Keep warm.

Turn hot rice out onto a platter, so that the crisp crust is on top. Serve hot saffron broth in a separate sauceboat or pitcher to pour over rice as desired. Serve immediately.

Serves 8

frenched string beans with sweet garlic sauce

"Frenching," or splitting beans lengthwise, adds a refined touch to a rather common vegetable; you can make this dish doubly elegant by using a combination of fresh green and yellow (wax) beans. Roasted garlic melts into a sweet, flavorful sauce enriched with the heart-healthy properties, and flavor, of extra-virgin olive oil. Happily the sauce can be made ahead of time, reheated briefly, and tossed with the beans.

1 large head **garlic**

1½ pounds **string beans**: a mixture of green and yellow

2 tablespoons plus 2 teaspoons **extra-virgin olive oil**

Preheat oven to 400°F.

Wrap garlic in a large piece of foil to make a pouch, and seal top tightly. Place in a pie tin and roast for 1 hour. Remove from oven. Cut garlic in half horizontally and squeeze out the pulp. Set aside.

Trim tips of beans. Wash thoroughly. Using a small sharp knife, cut beans in half lengthwise, following the seam of the bean.

Bring a large pot of salted water to a boil. Add beans and cook over high heat for 8 minutes, until tender.

Meanwhile, heat oil in a small skillet. Add 2 tablespoons garlic pulp and stir until garlic dissolves. Add 3 tablespoons boiling water from the beans and cook for 1 minute, until sauce thickens a little. Set aside.

Immediately drain beans in a colander, shaking off excess water. Place hot beans in a bowl and toss with garlic sauce that has been briefly reheated. Add kosher salt and freshly ground black pepper to taste. Stir to coat beans thoroughly. Serve hot.

Serves 6

Mixed Berry Shrub • Watermelon Splash • Cucumber-Mar

Shake • Iced Green Tea with Lemongrass Infusion • Blueberry-B

Tea • Wise Woman Sage Tea • White "Tea" • Lemon Balm So

Chamomile Tea with Lavender • Spiced "Coffee" • Ginser

Tonic • Pomegranate Lemonade • Strawberry-Coconut

na Smoothie • Tropical Soy Frullato • "Penicillin" • Immune

r • Laughing "Milk" • Green Apple Tisane with Tarragon •

ea with Maple-Ginger Essence • Strawberry-Basil Elixir

restoratives

Hot or cold, savory or mildly sweet, these smart drinks can lift your mood, settle your stomach, provide vitamins and minerals, boost your immune defenses, and allow for a quick time-out to relieve a bout of stress.

With the exception of green tea, which contains low levels of caffeine (but delivers incredible health benefits), some of the following beverages can stimulate your system more beneficially than a jolt of java, and without the jitterbugging.

These drinks also encourage spiritual nourishment. The simple ritual of preparing them, once or twice a day, to be drunk in quiet solitude or to be intimately shared, restores a sense of balance and awareness.

Some ingredients might be new to you, but discovery is the best part of self-growth. You'll have to visit an Asian market or a health food shop to find kombu, a dried sea vegetable, but who knows what else you'll encounter there; exotic pomegranate molasses can be found in Middle Eastern stores and, sometimes, in gourmet shops; stalks of fresh lemongrass now nestle in the produce section of many supermarkets; soy milk and buttermilk have become familiar presences in my fridge; and the differences among honeys (our planet sustains more than three hundred varieties) are revelations of their own.

To any of these drinks you can add a sprinkling of toasted wheat germ, a squirt of echinacea, a dash of cayenne pepper, a splash of olive-leaf extract, a spoonful of protein powder, or a drop of dewy wheat-grass juice.

mixed berry shrub

low calorie & fat-free

Here's an old-fashioned refreshment made with fruit, vinegar, and a sweetener for balance. In my update, balsamic vinegar is tempered by wildflower honey. This is so thick and flavorful that I often serve it instead of dessert, with a spoon.

16-ounce package frozen unsweetened **mixed berries**

6 tablespoons **wildflower honey**

3 tablespoons **balsamic vinegar**

Place frozen berries in a blender with 3 cups cold water. You may need to do this in 2 batches. Process on high until smooth. Add honey and balsamic vinegar and continue to blend until thick and very smooth. Serve immediately or keep chilled in refrigerator. Stir briskly, or shake, before serving. Serve in tall glasses or wine glasses.
Serves 6 (makes about 6½ cups)

watermelon splash

low calorie & fat-free

Cooling and soothing on a hot summer day, watermelon is packed with antioxidants and fresh mint leaves are said to calm the nerves. Serve this nonalcoholic refresher with hors d'oeuvres or for an afternoon tea.

1 pound ripe red **watermelon flesh**

2 cups unsweetened **pineapple juice**, chilled

1 small bunch fresh **mint**

Remove seeds and cut watermelon into chunks; place in freezer for about 1 hour, until frozen.

Transfer watermelon to a blender. Add pineapple juice and 2 tablespoons coarsely torn mint leaves. Process until very smooth. Garnish with remaining mint leaves.
Serves 4 (makes about 4½ cups)

cucumber-mango tonic

Cukes, mango, and lime make a revitalizing quaff that is especially hip served in an oversized martini glass. A New-Age alternative to the Margarita—nonalcoholic and vitamin rich.

4 **kirby cucumbers** (see Note)

12 ounces **mango nectar** (see Note)

2 **limes**

Peel cucumbers and cut into chunks. Place in a blender and process until very smooth.

Add mango nectar and the juice of 1 lime, about 3 tablespoons. Process until smooth.

Refrigerate until cold. Before serving, stir vigorously or shake well. Serve in chilled martini glasses garnished with wedges of the remaining lime.
Serves 4 (makes about 4 cups)

Note: If Kirby cucumbers are not available, use half of an English hothouse cucumber. Peel and scoop out seeds before processing. Mango nectar is readily available at health food stores and many grocery stores.

pomegranate lemonade

The ancients believed that pomegranate was an aphrodisiac and that it purged the system of envy and the taste for vengeance. On the verge of being trendy, pomegranate molasses is a lip-smacking reduction of pomegranate juice, and imparts a rose-colored hue.

¾ cup **sugar**

2 tablespoons **pomegranate molasses** (see Note)

5 large **lemons**

Combine sugar, 1 cup water, and pomegranate molasses in a medium saucepan. Mix well and bring to a boil. Lower heat and simmer for 1 minute. Let cool.

Meanwhile, cut 4 lemons in half and squeeze ⅔ cup juice. Add juice and 4 cups cold water to cooled pomegranate molasses mixture. Stir and refrigerate until cold.

Serve over ice and garnish with thin slices of remaining lemon.
Serves 6 (makes 6 cups)

Note: Pomegranate molasses is available in Middle Eastern and specialty food markets.

strawberry-coconut shake

Freezing super-ripe strawberries is the trick behind this shake's flavor and body. Coconut milk, now available lightened, provides an alluring flavor note and makes this drink low fat in addition to low cal. Serve with cookies (see pages 198 and 204) for an afternoon pick-me-up.

1 pint very ripe fresh **strawberries** or 12 ounces individually frozen strawberries

1 cup light **coconut milk**

¼ cup **sugar** or vanilla sugar (page 15)

If using fresh strawberries, wash thoroughly in a colander. Remove green stems and place berries in freezer until hard.

Place frozen berries in a blender. Add coconut milk, sugar, and 1 cup cold water. Process until very smooth.

Serves 4 (makes about 3¾ cups)

iced green tea with lemongrass infusion

We in the West are only beginning to appreciate the curative qualities of green tea, something every Asian doctor has known for ages. Now the drink of our future, green tea is a powerful antioxidant. It appears to protect against cancer and may help lower cholesterol. Green tea contains hundreds of phytochemicals, and no one yet knows exactly which deserve the credit. Slender stalks of lemongrass can be found in Asian markets and in the produce section of many supermarkets. This is a terrific drink to accompany lighter-style meals.

3 stalks **lemongrass**

2 tablespoons **honey**

2 tablespoons **Japanese green tea leaves** (sen-cha)

Remove tough outer leaves from 2 stalks of lemongrass. Finely chop lemongrass stalks, including the darker tops.

Bring 4¼ cups water, chopped lemongrass, and honey to a rapid boil. Lower heat and simmer for 10 minutes.

Place green tea leaves in a heatproof pitcher. Pour lemongrass infusion over the leaves and let steep for 2 minutes. (If you leave it longer the tea becomes bitter.)

Strain through a fine-mesh sieve. Cut remaining lemongrass stalk in half lengthwise, then crosswise. Let sit in tea until cool. Refrigerate until very cold. Serve over ice, garnished with a lemongrass stick.

Serves 4 (makes about 4 cups)

LEFT TO RIGHT:
Iced Green Tea with Lemongrass Infusion (above);
Blueberry-Banana Smoothie (page 158);
Cucumber-Mango Tonic (page 154)

blueberry-banana smoothie

Bananas and blueberries are big on fiber and potassium and, combined with yogurt, make an ultra-smooth tonic. This is a perfect way to start your day.

½ pint **blueberries**, fresh or frozen

1 ripe medium-large **banana**

8 ounces **nonfat vanilla yogurt**

If using fresh blueberries, wash thoroughly in a colander. Place in freezer until hard, about 1½ hours.

Place frozen berries in a blender. Peel banana and cut into ½-inch-thick slices. Add to blender with yogurt, 6 ice cubes, and ¼ cup cold water. Process on high until very smooth. Mixture will be thick and creamy. Add a little more water if necessary.

Serves 3 or 4 (makes 3 cups)

tropical soy frullato

I've become a convert to soy milk, largely because one dairy-free glass gives me 30 percent of my calcium requirement with zero saturated fat. (Do check the label, as this amount can vary, depending on the brand.) Add mango for its high fiber, and pineapple as a digestive aid and you've got an unbeatable beverage.

½ fresh ripe **pineapple**, about 1 pound trimmed

1 ripe **mango**

2 cups **vanilla soy milk**, chilled

Remove core and all rind from pineapple. Cut pineapple into 1-inch pieces and freeze for several hours until hard.

When ready to serve, remove skin from mango using a small sharp knife. Cut away mango flesh from pit and cut into small pieces. Place mango pieces in a blender. Add soy milk and frozen pineapple chunks. Process until thick and very smooth. Serve immediately in chilled wine glasses, or refrigerate until ready to use.

Serves 4 (makes about 6 cups)

"penicillin"

Scallions and sherry magically transform the most elemental of chicken broths into a multi-dimensional palliative that our grandmothers would have loved.

3 pounds **chicken wings**

3 **scallions**

1 tablespoon **dry sherry**

Using a cleaver, hack wings into several pieces to expose bones.

Place chicken pieces in a medium pot with enough cold water to cover by 1 inch. Thinly slice 2 scallions and add to pot, along with ½ teaspoon kosher salt and ¼ teaspoon white peppercorns.

Bring to a boil. Lower heat and cover pot. Cook over medium heat for 1½ hours.

Strain soup through a fine-mesh sieve into a clean pot. (You will have approximately 5½ cups at this point. Remove chicken. Save for another use. Continue to cook broth over medium heat until reduced to 4 cups, about 20 minutes.

Remove as much fat as possible. If using later, chill, skim fat, and reheat. Add sherry and remaining scallion that has been thinly sliced. Cook for 5 minutes. Serve in large mugs.
Serves 4 (makes about 4 cups)

immune tea

This has a haunting taste of the sea. Kombu, like most sea vegetables, contains a rich array of trace minerals and is an excellent source of nondairy calcium. Shiitake mushrooms have been used in Asia as food and medicine for thousands of years. Sip and savor at the first sign of sniffles, or when you just need some quiet time.

½ ounce **kombu** (see Note)

4 or 5 **dried shiitake mushrooms**, about ¼ ounce

Fresh **cilantro** leaves

Break up kombu into 1-inch pieces and place in a bowl or pitcher. Add shiitake mushrooms and cover with 4½ cups cold water. Let sit for 1 hour.

Transfer kombu, mushrooms, and soaking liquid to a saucepan. Bring just to a boil but do not let boil. Remove kombu with a slotted spoon and simmer for 1 minute.

Remove shiitakes from tea. Cut stems from caps and discard stems. Slice caps thinly.

Pour tea into warm mugs. Garnish with sliced mushrooms and a few torn or finely julienned leaves of cilantro. Serve hot.
Serves 4 (makes about 4 cups)

Note: Kombu is a sun-dried Japanese sea vegetable commonly used to make stock, basic to Japanese cuisine. It comes packaged and is available in health food stores and Asian food markets.

wise woman sage tea

Sage comes from the Latin word *salvia,* which means "savior," but also connotes "safe, whole, and healthy." Sage, an antiseptic, is a wise choice for appeasing colds.

¼ cup good-quality dried **sage** leaves (see Note)

2 tablespoons best-quality **honey**: clover, leatherwood, or wildflower

1 **lemon**, thinly sliced

Place sage leaves in a heatproof pitcher or teapot. Bring 5 cups water to a boil and pour over sage leaves. Add honey and lemon slices. Let steep for 10 to 15 minutes. Strain through a fine-mesh sieve or tea strainer directly into warm cups or reheat gently. Serve with a slice of lemon.
Serves 4 (makes about 4¾ cups)

Note: Dried sage is best purchased from a Middle Eastern or spice store.

white "tea"

This sugar-and-spice beverage gets its sweetness and heady flavor from milky almond syrup. Its two warming spices, stick cinnamon and the more exotic star anise, are said to be good for chills and joint stiffness and for relieving a touch of nausea and bloating.

⅓ cup **orgeat syrup** (almond syrup; see Note)

2 sticks **cinnamon**

5 **star anise**

Place 4 cups water in a medium saucepan. Add almond syrup, cinnamon sticks, and anise. Bring to a boil. Lower heat and simmer for 10 minutes.

Strain through a fine-mesh sieve into 4 teacups. Using a small sharp knife, split cinnamon sticks in half lengthwise and use to garnish each serving.
Serves 4 (makes about 4 cups)

Note: Orgeat syrup, also known as orzata, is available in Italian markets and specialty food stores.

lemon balm soother

Lemon balm is indeed a balm, drunk to lift one's spirit from winter doldrums. Fresh lime juice adds vitamin C and other antimicrobial activity to the brew, with honey to soothe.

¼ heaping cup dried **lemon balm** or lemon verbena leaves

3 tablespoons **honey**

2 small **limes**

Place lemon balm or lemon verbena in a heatproof pitcher or teapot. Place 4 cups water and honey in a saucepan and bring to a boil. Pour over lemon balm and add a lime that has been thinly sliced. Let steep, covered, for 25 minutes, then strain into saucepan. Reheat gently and serve in warmed teacups. Garnish with remaining lime that has been sliced paper-thin.

Serves 4 (makes about 4 cups)

laughing "milk"

In Shirley King's translation of *Pampille's Table: Recipes from the French Countryside,* this drink is known as *poule* (chicken) milk, offered with the following directive: "Take to the bedroom of a child with a cold. It will make his cold better, and it will amuse him to drink it." Milk-like yet dairy-free.

1 **egg yolk**

1½ tablespoons **sugar**

¼ teaspoon **orange-flower water** (see Note)

Place egg yolk in a bowl and whisk in sugar. Bring 1 cup of water to a boil and add orange-flower water.

Gradually whisk boiling water mixture into egg mixture, then whisk vigorously so that drink has foamy top and egg and sugar are completely incorporated. Mixture will look like milk. Serve immediately.

Serves 1 (makes 1 cup with foam)

Note: Orange-flower water is a distillate of bitter orange flowers, available in small blue bottles in Middle Eastern and specialty food shops.

green apple tisane with tarragon

If grandmother was right about chicken soup, she also was correct about the virtues of an apple a day. Apples contain phenolic acids and flavonoids, phytochemicals that appear to protect your heart. Refreshingly tart and aromatic after a filling meal.

1 medium **Granny Smith apple**

1 teaspoon dried **tarragon** leaves

1 tablespoon plus 2 teaspoons fragrant **honey**: acacia or orange blossom

Wash apple but do not peel. Cut apple in half. Remove seeds and cut into thin wedges. Put 2½ cups water, tarragon leaves, honey, and apple wedges in a medium saucepan. Bring to a boil. Lower heat to medium and cook for 15 minutes, breaking up apples with a spoon.

Strain through a fine-mesh sieve, pressing down hard on the apples to extract all the juice.

Serve hot in mugs; alternatively, refrigerate until cold and serve over ice.

Serves 2 (makes about 2 ½ cups)

TOP TO BOTTOM:
Spiced "Coffee" (page 164);
Green Apple Tisane with Tarragon (above);
Strawberry-Basil Elixir (page 165);
Ginseng Tea with Maple-Ginger Essence (page 165)

chamomile tea with lavender

low calorie & fat-free

Chamomile is a mainstay of European folk medicine and is a good home remedy for upset stomachs. Herbalists say that chamomile and lavender can ease insomnia because of their relaxant properties. Their dried flowers are available in spice shops and often in natural food stores.

2 tablespoons dried chamomile flowers or 2 **chamomile tea bags**

1 teaspoon **dried lavender flowers**

2 teaspoons **sugar**

Place chamomile flowers or tea bags, lavender flowers, and sugar in a teapot.

Bring 2 ¼ cups water to a rapid boil in a small saucepan and pour into teapot. Let steep for 15 minutes, covered, then strain into warmed teacups. Alternatively, chill tea and serve over ice.

Serves 2 (makes 2 cups)

spiced "coffee"

low calorie & fat-free

Blackstrap molasses (the last extraction from the cane when refining sugar) is high in iron, potassium, magnesium, and calcium. Citrus peel, whether orange or tangerine, contains monoterpenes, phytochemicals that may help detoxify carcinogens. Pretty stimulating for a no-caffeine brew—and a satisfying fillip at the end of a meal.

3 tablespoons unsulphured **molasses**

2 teaspoons **pickling spice**

4 long strips tangerine or **orange rind**

Place 3 cups water in a medium saucepan. Add molasses, pickling spice, and rind. Bring to a boil. Lower heat to maintain a simmer and cook for 5 minutes. Strain through a fine-mesh sieve into 4 coffee cups. Garnish with strips of rind. To serve later, leave rind in strained "coffee" and reheat gently.

Serves 4 (makes about 3 cups)

ginseng tea with maple-ginger essence

Ginseng is a sweet licorice-flavored root whose botanical name, *panax*, is derived from the Greek word panacea, meaning all-healing. Whether the warmest Chinese red or the cooler American variety, ginseng is believed, in many circles, to invigorate the immune, endocrine, and nervous systems. It should be steeped for at least an hour to release its riches.

2-inch piece fresh **ginger**

3 tablespoons real **maple syrup**

½ ounce **ginseng root** (see Note)

Peel ginger and slice into paper-thin coins.

Bring 4¼ cups water, ginger slices, and maple syrup to a boil. Lower heat, add ginseng, and simmer for 15 minutes.

Transfer, with ginseng and ginger, to a heatproof pitcher. Let steep for about 1 hour.

Remove the ginger and the ginseng, which you may reuse (see Note). Reheat tea gently.

Strain hot tea into 4 warmed cups and serve immediately.
Serves 4 (makes about 4 cups)

Note: Ginseng is available in health food stores and many supermarkets. To reuse ginseng, let dry completely. Store in a cool dry place. Ginseng may be used repeatedly until there is no flavor left in the pieces.

strawberry-basil elixir

Strawberries have high levels of vitamin C and beneficial phytochemicals. Crushed, then steeped, they make a beautiful pink tincture, heady with the aroma of basil. Great for sipping in a hot tub.

1 pint ripe **strawberries**, about 12 ounces

2 tablespoons **sugar**

2 tablespoons dried **basil** leaves

Wash berries and pat dry. Remove green stems from all but 4 berries.

Place hulled berries and sugar in bowl of a food processor and process until strawberries are broken up into small pieces and become a kind of chunky puree. You will have about 1½ cups.

Transfer to a heatproof pitcher. Stir in basil leaves.

Bring 4 cups water to a rapid boil and pour over strawberry-basil mixture. Let steep for 15 minutes. Strain through a coarse-mesh sieve directly into warm cups or reheat gently. Garnish each with a strawberry, split halfway through and placed on rim of cup.
Serves 4 (makes about 4 ¼ cups)

Fresh Blueberries and Blueberry Compote, Lemon "Custard" • Fresh Apricots in Cinn

Dust • Raspberry-Honey Fool • Peaches in Peach Schnapps with Basil • Mangoes a

Melon Balls, Mint, and Lime Oil • Watermelon "Carpaccio" with White Chocolate • Can

• Poached Seckel Pears, Maple-Cardamom Syrup • Prunes and Chocolate, Port Wine S

Candied Violets • Crown of Green Figs and Raspberries, Rock

Terrine with Giant Strawberries, Pineapple Syrup • Rosem

Tarragon, Almond Sorbetto • Baked Sabra Oranges, Chocola

• Poached Pineapple in Red Honey Syrup, Rose Hips Sorbet

• Strawberry-Ginger Sorbet, Macerated Berries and Ginger C

with Walnut Crunch, Red Plum Sauce • Orange Gratin with

Vanilla Yogurt Timbale • Cider-Poached Apples, Cider Syrup and Swirls of Cream •

Mousse Sponge • A Simple Vanilla Gâteau • Cinnamon Chocolate Ciambell

Cheese with Roasted Grapes • Brie and Seckel Pear, Dried Figs • Cantalou

and Mint • Bosc Pear and Parmigiano-Reggiano, Melon Liqueur • Stilto

on Syrup • Pineapple Shingles with Caramel, Pistachio
Blackberries, Blackberry Coulis • "Canary" Soup with
oupe and Raspberries, Melba Sauce and Melon Ribbons
ce • 1-2-3 Fruit Soup • Pink Grapefruit in Guava Nectar,
gar and Fig Coulis • Melon au Porto • Yogurt "Cheese"
-Poached Pears "Vino Cotto" • Turkish Apricots with
Orange Sorbet • Anjou Pears and Grappa, Pear Granita
Red and White Cherry Soup with Star Anise, Cherry Ice
s • Frosted Lemons with Yogurt Gelato • Baked Plums
neapple-Orange Sabayon • Warm Rhubarb Compote,
ench Walnut Torte • Cocoa Meringues • Chocolate
• Cinnamon-Sugar Crisps • Biscottini • Cabrales
with Manchego and Honey • Watermelon, Feta,
Cheese with Roasted Lady Apples, Port Syrup

fruits and desserts

Dessert

Dessert used to be a reward for finishing your vegetables—but today this end-of-meal flourish has its own nutritional excuse for being.

A familiar lament among the calorically challenged—that "everything's fattening"—applies particularly to the jubilation brought on by dessert's irresistibility. So here is sweetness and "lite": all of these desserts are either fat-free, low fat, or low calorie and most, amazingly, are both fat-free or low fat *and* low calorie.

You can forget your fear of "empty calories," because most desserts in this chapter rely on fruit for their flavor, their sweet-acid notes, their bold strokes of color, and their nutritive value. If nutritional labels were glued to these recipes, sugar (if present at all) would appear last on the list of ingredients.

At the restaurant Troisgros, in France, I once was mesmerized by a thin apple tart baked with tarragon, and have been experimenting ever since with combinations of fruit and fresh herbs and spices. So in this chapter you'll find peaches with basil, rosemary-poached pears, cherry soup with star anise, and seckel pears in cardamom syrup.

Even sophisticated combinations of fruit with cheese (yes!) have a place in this healthy 1-2-3 parade. For aficionados of the cocoa bean there are chocolate mousse sponge, prunes and chocolate in port wine sauce, cinnamon-chocolate *ciambella,* and cocoa meringues, all of which induce guiltless euphoria.

But nowhere is my philosophy more magically expressed than in baking a cake with only three ingredients. Many of us, put off by fear of complexity, avoid baking cakes, so I've included several simple, enlightened beauties that just beg for time in your oven.

Perhaps most encouraging, there's nothing artificial in any of this chapter's recipes, and no pink or blue packages to open.

low calorie & low fat

fresh blueberries and blueberry compote, lemon "custard"

Conventional wisdom says that blue is not a good color for food. Nonsense! Blueberries have gained a reputation as the "wonder fruit" for their anthocyanins, the natural dyes in food revered for their antioxidant prowess.

2 pints fresh, large **blueberries**

3 tablespoons **sugar**

6 ounces **low-fat lemon yogurt** (see Note)

Wash berries in a colander under cold running water. Remove any stems. Dry thoroughly and transfer to a bowl. Place 1 cup blueberries in a saucepan with 3 tablespoons sugar and ½ cup water. Bring to a boil. Lower heat to medium-low and cook for 20 minutes, stirring often. Remove from heat. Let cool for 10 minutes and pour over remaining berries in bowl. Mix gently. Refrigerate for several hours or until cold.

Freeze 4 wine glasses. When ready to serve, carefully spoon berry mixture into frozen wine glasses. Dollop with yogurt and top with a few blueberries.
Serves 4

Note: Yoplait makes a good one called Lemon Supreme.

low calorie & fat-free

fresh apricots in cinnamon syrup

Apricots originated in China, where they are poetically named "moon of the faithful." Their beautiful yellow-orange hue tells you these small stone fruits are powered with beta-carotene. Chinese herbalists are more poetic: they say that cinnamon twigs are like the streets of a city, branching out and carrying their beneficial effects to every part of the body.

15 firm **apricots**, about 2 pounds

5 tablespoons **dark brown sugar**

4 sticks **cinnamon**

Wash apricots. Cut in half and remove stones.

In a 4-quart saucepan, put 2 cups water, brown sugar, cinnamon, ¼ teaspoon black peppercorns, and a pinch of salt. Bring to a boil.

Lower heat to medium. Add apricots and cook over medium heat for 10 minutes. Let cool. Remove apricots with slotted spoon.

Cook juices over high heat for a few minutes until reduced and syrupy. Pour over apricots. Chill until very cold.
Serves 6

pineapple shingles with caramel, pistachio dust

The Spanish named pineapple "pina" because of its pinecone shape, which so frightened Emperor Charles V that he refused to taste it. Pity, since fresh pineapple contains an enzyme that breaks down proteins and contributes to healthy digestion. Pistachios provide vitamins and a little "healthy" fat. Together, they make a fragrantly forward dessert, under a web of caramel candy.

1 very ripe medium **pineapple**

¼ cup shelled unsalted **pistachios**, about 1 ounce

4 tablespoons plus 1 teaspoon **sugar**

Remove rind from pineapple, removing all "eyes" and dark brown spots. Cut into 4 wedges, cutting away the hard woody core.

Cut wedges lengthwise into ⅛-inch-thick slices to create "shingles." Place slices, tightly overlapping, in the centers of 4 large plates.

Lightly toast pistachios in a small nonstick skillet. Let cool completely. Process in food processor until finely ground. Set aside.

Wipe out the skillet. Add sugar and cook over high heat, stirring constantly with a wooden spoon, until sugar melts and becomes a dark brown caramel syrup. Immediately drizzle caramel in a lacy pattern evenly over pineapple. Let cool for 1 minute. Caramel will harden and become brittle.

Dust perimeter of pineapple and the plate with ground pistachios. Serve immediately.

Serves 4

raspberry-honey fool

Brought to America by the Brits, a fool is a "pud" made of stewed fruit and sweetened whipped cream. My version is lighter and more nutritious: it sheds lots of sugar and substitutes healthful yogurt for the cream. If you want to fool around, try making this with fleshy ripe persimmons.

2½ pints fresh **raspberries**

5 tablespoons aromatic **honey**: leatherwood, wild thyme, or buckwheat

2 cups **nonfat plain yogurt**

Wash berries and dry thoroughly.

Place 1 cup water, 3 tablespoons honey, and ½ pint berries in a small saucepan. Bring to a boil. Lower heat to medium and cook for 15 minutes, pressing down on raspberries to extract as much flavor as possible.

Strain through a coarse-mesh sieve, again pressing down on berries, and return syrup to saucepan. Cook over high heat until reduced to ½ cup. Let cool and refrigerate until cold.

In a small bowl mix yogurt and 2 tablespoons honey, then refrigerate until ready to serve.

In the bottom of each of 4 large wine glasses place some washed berries. Add ¼ cup yogurt, 1 tablespoon syrup, more raspberries, another ¼ cup yogurt, 1 tablespoon syrup, and finish with some more berries. Serve immediately.
Serves 4

peaches in peach schnapps with basil

This fat-free marriage of flavors is so hip, you'll never want peaches and cream again. And a little schnapps, according to Jewish tradition, couldn't hurt.

6 large, firm ripe **peaches**

½ cup **peach schnapps**

1 bunch fresh **basil**

Bring a medium pot of water to a boil. Add peaches. Lower heat to medium and cook for 5 to 10 minutes, depending on firmness of peaches. They should be soft but still retain their shape.

Remove peaches with a slotted spoon. Carefully peel off skin. Cut peaches in half and remove pits. Place 3 halves in each of 4 large wine goblets.

In a small saucepan put schnapps, ½ cup water, and several sprigs of fresh basil. Bring to a boil. Boil for 2 minutes. Let cool. Remove basil and discard.

Apportion liquid evenly over peaches. Refrigerate until very cold. Garnish with fresh basil sprigs.
Serves 4

fat-free

mangoes and blackberries, blackberry coulis

Juicy tropical mangoes burst with beta-carotene and vitamin C; fleshy sweet blackberries are flush with calcium. This is an easy but elegant dessert you can serve with confidence.

2 large ripe **mangoes**

2 pints ripe **blackberries**

¼ cup **sugar**

Using a small sharp knife, cut skin from mangoes. Cut each mango in half, cutting flesh away from the large center pit. Cut each half into long ½-inch-thick slices. Place in refrigerator until ready to serve.

Wash berries. Place 1 cup berries in a saucepan with 1¼ cups water and sugar. Bring to a boil. Lower heat to medium and cook for 15 minutes, pressing down firmly on berries with a spoon. Strain coulis through a coarse mesh sieve. Let syrup cool.

Place mango slices in a pinwheel fashion on each of 4 large plates.

Place 6 or 7 fresh berries in center of each plate. Spoon coulis carefully between mango slices. Serve immediately.
Serves 4

low calorie & low fat

"canary" soup with melon balls, mint, and lime oil

A "canary" is a particularly luscious melon with a pronounced perfume. For this dessert, a pyramid of melon balls rises from a puddle of lime-spiked melon puree. A pinch of salt makes the flavors reverberate. If you can't find pure lime oil, substitute fresh lime juice and a little grated zest; if you can't find canary melon, casaba, Crenshaw, galia, or honeydew will do.

1 large ripe **canary melon**, about 4 pounds

1 large bunch **mint,** enough to yield ¼ cup plus additional leaves for garnish

¼ teaspoon **lime oil** (see Note)

Cut melon in half through the stem end. Scoop out seeds. Remove rind from one half using a small sharp knife, then cut into large chunks. Place in bowl of a food processor. Wash mint and chop ¼ cup. Add to processor. Process for several minutes, until very smooth. Transfer to a bowl. Whisk in lime oil. Cover and refrigerate until very cold. Makes 3 cups.

Using a small melon baller, scoop out balls from remaining half. Place in another small bowl. Add any accumulated juices to the bowl with soup. Chill thoroughly.

Ladle soup into 4 chilled shallow soup bowls. Place a mound of melon balls in center. Garnish with sprigs of fresh mint.
Serves 4

Note: Use all-natural pure lime oil from Boyajian, available in many specialty food stores and stores specializing in baking equipment and products. You may substitute ½ teaspoon freshly grated lime zest and 1 or more tablespoons fresh lime juice.

watermelon "carpaccio" with white chocolate

This dessert whimsically mimics the famous carpaccio served at Harry's Bar in Venice. Here, paper-thin slices of watermelon, whose color is deepened by a splash of purple crème de cassis, stand in for raw beef, while shards of white chocolate look a lot like wafers of parmesan cheese.

1 large wedge seedless red **watermelon**, 1 pound edible portion

2 tablespoons **crème de cassis** or black currant syrup

2½-ounce chunk **white chocolate** at room temperature

Remove rind from watermelon. Cut into slices about ⅛ inch thick. Line the interior of 4 serving plates with watermelon slices. Trim the perimeter evenly to make a circle. Remove seeds, if any.

Drizzle each plate with ½ tablespoon crème de cassis.

Let white chocolate get warm enough, leaving at room temperature, so that you can make paper-thin slices (that will curl up a bit) using a sharp vegetable peeler or cheese slicer. They should resemble shards of parmesan cheese.

Scatter over watermelon and serve immediately.

Serves 4

cantaloupe and raspberries, melba sauce and melon ribbons

This confection resembles a birthday treat. Gumdrop-shaped raspberries sit atop a "cake" of finely diced cantaloupe decorated with colorful raspberry puree and ribbons of melon. Gifts for the body include beta-carotene, vitamin C, potassium, and soluble fiber.

2 pints **raspberries**

2½ tablespoons **sugar**

1 large ripe **cantaloupe**

Wash berries. Place ½ pint berries in a small saucepan with 1 cup water and sugar. Bring to a boil. Lower heat and simmer for 15 minutes. Strain through a coarse-mesh sieve, pressing down firmly on the berries to release all the liquid. You will have about ½ cup. Let cool.

Using a sharp knife, remove rind from melon. Cut three-quarters of the melon into ¼-inch-thick slices. Remove all seeds. Dice into ¼-inch cubes. Pack diced melon into a 4-inch ring mold on each of 4 large plates, pressing down firmly to make a "cake." Remove ring. Place remaining uncooked raspberries to cover the top of each (about 16 raspberries).

Using a vegetable peeler, make wide ribbons from remaining quarter of melon.

Spoon 2 tablespoons of raspberry sauce around each "cake." Place folded melon ribbons on the sauce around each cake.
Serves 4

poached seckel pears, maple-cardamom syrup

Seckel pears, a small American variety with a spicy flavor, simmer, then shimmer like tiny ornaments in an aromatic glaze. The boiled down sap of the sugar maple tree is boiled again here with fragrant pods of exotic cardamom, traditionally used in India to aid digestion and sweeten the breath.

18 seckel **pears** with stems, about 2¼ pounds

½ cup real **maple syrup**

16 green **cardamom pods** (see Note)

Wash pears, leaving stems attached. Do not peel.

In a medium pot, put 6 cups water, maple syrup, and a pinch of kosher salt. Using the side of a large heavy knife, crack cardamom pods and add to pot. Bring to a boil.

Add pears and return to a boil. Place cover askew. Lower heat and simmer for 30 minutes. The pears should be tender but still retain their shape.

Remove pears with a slotted spoon and place in a shallow bowl.

Over high heat, cook until liquid is reduced to about 1¼ cups, about 15 to 20 minutes. Pour over pears and refrigerate until very cold.
Serves 6

Note: Green cardamom pods are available in Middle Eastern food stores and spice markets.

prunes and chocolate, port wine sauce

This is a sensory exploration of sweet and bitter, for there's lots of both in port and chocolate. In addition to their laxative notoriety, prunes are rich in blood-building iron, potassium, and fiber. Port offers the heart-protective compounds found in all red wine. And high-quality dark chocolate is known to contain beneficial phytochemicals.

24 large **prunes** with pits, about 1 pound

1 cup **tawny port**

2-ounce chunk semisweet **chocolate** at room temperature

Cook prunes in a saucepan with enough water to cover for 20 minutes over medium heat. Let cool in liquid. Refrigerate overnight.

Remove 1 cup prune liquid and place in a small saucepan. Cook over medium-high heat until reduced to ½ cup. Pour in a small bowl and chill.

Wipe out saucepan and add port. Cook over medium-high heat until reduced to ½ cup. Chill.

When ready to serve, place 6 prunes in each of 4 shallow soup bowls. Spoon over 2 tablespoons reduced prune juice and 2 tablespoons reduced port.

Leave chocolate at room temperature so that it is warm enough to slice. Cut chocolate into thin julienne. Scatter over prunes. Serve immediately.
Serves 4

1-2-3 fruit soup

The renowned culinarian Curnonsky proclaimed "cuisine is when things taste like themselves." This, then, must certainly be it: three fragrant fruits, simply pureed and presented in swirls of pink, coral, and green. Together they contribute an abundance of beta-carotene, vitamin C, and potassium.

1 medium very ripe **cantaloupe**, about 1½ pounds

½ large very ripe **honeydew**, about 1½ pounds

1½-pound chunk of red **watermelon** with seeds

Remove rind and any seeds from cantaloupe and cut into chunks. Place in bowl of food processor with 2 tablespoons water. Process with a small pinch of kosher salt until very smooth. You will have 2 cups of liquid. Place in a small pitcher. Repeat process with honeydew. Place in a separate pitcher.

Remove seeds from watermelon and save 12 as a garnish. Discard all others. Process two-thirds of the watermelon (do not add any water) and place in another pitcher. Refrigerate all three for at least 4 hours. The juices will thicken as they sit.

Using a quenelle-shaped ice cream scoop (or a small round scoop) scoop out 4 ovals (or balls) from remaining watermelon.

Before serving, chill 4 large flat soup plates.

When ready to serve, carefully, quickly, and almost simultaneously pour each puree (about ½ cup) into a third of each plate, trying to keep the colors as separate as possible (you can ask a friend to lend a "third" hand). They will flow together. Place watermelon oval or ball in center of each bowl. Garnish with a few seeds. Serve immediately.
Serves 4

pink grapefruit in guava nectar, candied violets

Guava nectar, reduced to a pink, sticky syrup, tastes like a tropical paradise when poured over equally pink grapefruit. You get lots of vitamin C, and these fruits are among the few non-tomato sources of lycopene, thought to reduce the risk of certain cancers. Candied violets are a frivolous touch, good for the spirit.

1⅔ cups **guava nectar** (one 11½-ounce can)

5 large **pink grapefruit**

1 ounce **candied violets**

Place guava nectar in a small saucepan. Bring to a boil. Lower heat to medium and cook until reduced to ¾ cup. Let cool. Chill until ready to use.

Using a sharp knife remove rind from grapefruits. Remove all white pith and cut along membranes to release segments.

Arrange segments in a circular fashion, touching but not overlapping, on each of 4 large plates, placing a few segments in center of circle.

Spoon 3 tablespoons guava reduction over grapefruit segments. Garnish with candied violets. *Serves 4*

fat-free

crown of green figs and raspberries, rock sugar and fig coulis

This is a late-summer marriage of tastes, when figs and raspberries are at their luscious best. The crowning glory: a flourish of fresh fig coulis and jewels of amber sugar. This is equally stunning made with fleshy purple figs.

6 **brown crystal rock sugar sticks**, about 2 ounces total (see Note)

20 small ripe green **figs**

2 pints fresh **raspberries**, about 12 ounces

In a small saucepan, place ¾ cup water and 1 whole stick of sugar. Bring to a boil. Boil until sugar melts; remove stick and discard. Let syrup cool, then refrigerate.

Wash figs and trim stems. Cut 6 figs in half and place in bowl of a food processor. Add ½ cup of the chilled sugar syrup and process until a smooth sauce is formed, adding more sugar syrup if needed. Chill until ready to serve.

Cut each remaining fig into 4 wedges. Wash raspberries and dry well.

On each of 4 large plates, outline a large circle with raspberries (about 20) with a diameter of about 5 inches. Fill the center with cut figs.

Use a sharp knife to cut sugar from remaining sticks, breaking them into small crystals. Scatter on figs. Drizzle a little fig sauce on the figs and on the plate, outside the raspberry circle. Serve within 30 minutes.

Serves 4

Note: Brown crystal rock sugar sticks can be found in many specialty food stores. They look like swizzle sticks half encrusted with sugar crystals. They often are used as stirrers to accompany hot beverages. Or you may be lucky enough to find packages of coarse brown sugar crystals in a specialty baking store.

melon au porto

Strikingly minimal, this simple dessert is a study in texture and flavor. Wedges of sweet honeydew arch around a translucent, slightly jiggly, ruby center made with full-bodied ruby port and gelatin. Strict vegetarians can make this with a natural, non-animal setting agent.

1 large, round ripe **honeydew**, about 3 pounds

1¾ cups **ruby port**

2 envelopes unflavored **gelatin**

Cut melon in half lengthwise through the stem end, and scoop out the seeds. Cut small straight slices from bottom of melon halves so that they sit perfectly level.

In a large saucepan, put port and 1¾ cups water. Sprinkle with gelatin. Let sit for 1 minute. Bring just to a boil, stirring constantly, until gelatin dissolves. Lower heat to maintain a simmer and cook for 5 minutes, stirring frequently. Let cool for 10 minutes.

Pour port mixture into melon halves, coming up to the top of the melon, reserving leftover port mixture. Carefully put filled melon halves in refrigerator. Chill for at least 4 hours, until very firm.

Pour remaining mixture into 6 small ramekins, custard cups, or decorative molds. Carefully put in refrigerator. Chill for at least 4 hours, until very firm.

Cut melon into 6 wedges. Place on plates. Unmold ramekins by dipping bottoms into boiling water for a few seconds. Place one next to each melon wedge and serve.

Serves 6

yogurt "cheese" terrine with giant strawberries, pineapple syrup

Startlingly white, red, and buttercup yellow, this dessert is composed of drained yogurt that forms a brick of thick "cheese." It sits in a pool of pineapple syrup, and is topped with a roof of red berries. Absorbable calcium, potassium, phosphorus, and good looks are but a few of this dessert's elemental benefits.

4 cups **nonfat plain yogurt**

2 cups unsweetened **pineapple juice**

30 to 36 large **strawberries**

Using a bamboo skewer, make 25 holes in the bottom of an 8½-by-4½-by-2½-inch foil loaf pan. Line the pan with cheesecloth so that it overhangs sides of pan by several inches all around. Spoon in yogurt, smoothing the top with a spatula. Tap on the counter to release any air bubbles. Place on a rack with a receptacle underneath to catch the liquid that drains. Fold overhanging cheesecloth over the top of the pan.

Let sit at room temperature for 6 hours, draining liquid from time to time. Then refrigerate for up to 24 hours, with receptacle underneath.

Several hours before serving, cook 1¾ cups pineapple juice over medium-high heat until reduced to 1 cup. Let cool. Chill until ready to use.

When ready to serve, unmold terrine, carefully turning loaf pan upside down on a platter. Carefully remove cheesecloth.

Wash berries and dry. Trim stem ends of berries with a small sharp knife so that they sit straight. Place berries, cut side down, on terrine so that they touch and cover top of terrine completely. In a small saucepan, cook remaining ¼ cup juice until reduced to a glaze, about 2 tablespoons. Using a pastry brush, coat berries with glaze.

Serve terrine surrounded by 1 cup chilled pineapple reduction.

Serves 6

rosemary-poached pears "vino cotto"

fat-free

A whole poached pear can indeed stand alone. But this pear stands out in "vino cotto," a syrupy reduction of white grape juice. Here it is perfumed and garnished with piney rosemary, once considered a memory-strengthening herb.

6 large, firm ripe **Comice pears** with stems

4 cups **white grape juice**

1 large bunch fresh **rosemary**

Using a sharp vegetable peeler, peel pears, leaving stems intact.

In a 4-quart pot, place pears, grape juice, 3 cups water (or more, to just cover pears), and 6 sprigs rosemary. Bring to a boil.

Cover pot and lower heat to medium. Cook for 30 minutes. Let pears cool in liquid.

Remove pears with a slotted spoon. Place in a dish. Cover and refrigerate.

Remove rosemary from liquid in pot. Bring liquid to a boil. Lower heat to medium and cook until liquid is reduced to 1¾ cups. Pour 1¼ cups reduced liquid over pears, adding a few sprigs of fresh rosemary. Cover and chill well.

Reduce remaining ½ cup liquid to a glaze (about 4 tablespoons). Let cool.

Serve pears, with poaching liquid, in shallow soup bowls. Garnish with sprigs of fresh rosemary. Spoon a little of the cooled glaze over the pears.
Serves 6

fruits and sorbets

turkish apricots with tarragon, almond sorbetto

fat-free

Here's another unusual pairing of fruit and herbs: the acid notes of dried apricots seem to sweeten under the influence of tarragon's subtle bouquet. Tarragon was once reputed to soothe snakebites, should the need arise. A sorbetto of highly perfumed almond syrup is the final note in this harmonious passage.

1 pound large **dried Turkish apricots**

⅔ cup **orgeat syrup** (almond syrup; see Note)

1 bunch **tarragon** leaves

Place apricots in a medium pot. Add 3 cups water and bring to a boil. Lower heat, cover, and simmer for 25 minutes. Pour ⅓ cup orgeat syrup over apricots. Add 10 to 12 tarragon leaves. Let cool. Refrigerate until very cold.

Place ⅓ cup orgeat syrup, 1½ cups water, and 4 cooked apricots in bowl of a food processor. Process until very smooth. Place in a shallow metal dish and freeze for several hours, scraping with a fork every 30 minutes to break up ice crystals.

When ready to serve, divide apricots and juices among 8 shallow soup bowls. Place almond ice in food processor and process until a smooth sorbet is formed.

Place a scoop of sorbet on top of apricots and garnish with fresh tarragon leaves.
Serves 8

Note: Orgeat syrup, also known as orzata, is available in Italian markets and specialty food stores.

baked sabra oranges, chocolate-orange sorbet

This dessert features a remarkable fruit compote *and* a flavor-packed sorbet—both infused with Sabra, a chocolate-orange liqueur from Israel. The chocolate essence darts right to your nostrils through the strong citrus perfume. You need to boil the oranges several times in fresh water to reduce bitterness from skins. You also need an ice-cream maker.

12 large thin-skinned juice **oranges**

1¾ cups **sugar**

7 tablespoons **Sabra liqueur**

Preheat oven to 375°F.

Wash 6 oranges and place in a medium-large pot. Cover with cold water and bring to a rapid boil. Boil for 20 minutes. Pour water off and cover oranges again with cold water. Bring to a boil and boil for 5 minutes. Remove oranges with a slotted spoon and place on a cutting board.

Cut each orange into 8 wedges and arrange, cut side down, in a 13-by-9-inch shallow casserole or glass baking dish large enough to accommodate oranges in 1 layer. In a small saucepan, bring 2 cups water and 1½ cups sugar to a boil. Boil for 1 minute, until sugar is dissolved, and pour over oranges.

Bake for 30 minutes. Turn oranges over and bake for 30 minutes longer. Remove from oven.

Pour 4 tablespoons Sabra over oranges. Let cool and refrigerate, covered, until very cold.

To make sorbet, grate rind of 1 or 2 oranges to yield 2 teaspoons grated zest. Cut remaining oranges in half and squeeze 2 cups juice. Place in a small bowl with orange zest and 3 tablespoons Sabra. In a small saucepan, bring ⅓ cup water and ¼ cup sugar to a boil and boil until sugar is dissolved. Add to bowl with orange juice.

Transfer juice mixture to a bowl and chill until very cold. Freeze in an ice-cream maker according to manufacturer's directions to make a smooth sorbet.

Serve cold oranges with syrup in shallow dessert dishes. Top with a scoop of sorbet.
Serves 8 (makes 3 cups sorbet)

anjou pears and grappa, pear granita

Anjous are winter pears and come in holiday colors of red and green. Grappa (a clear Italian brandy made from grape skins and pips) is traditionally a heart-warming winter drink. Together they unite in a fat-free adult dessert with a high flavor profile and respectable quantities of fiber.

1⅔ cups **pear nectar**

6 tablespoons **grappa**

4 large ripe **Anjou pears** (2 green and 2 red if possible)

In a small bowl, mix pear nectar and 3 tablespoons grappa. Place in a shallow metal pan and place in freezer. Scrape with a fork every 30 minutes to break up ice crystals. Continue for 2 to 3 hours, until frozen but still just a little slushy.

Just before serving, wash pears and dry thoroughly. Cut into long thin wedges, removing the core and seeds. Place in a bowl. Toss quickly with remaining grappa.

Immediately place pears in 4 large wine glasses. Top with pear granita. Add a coarse grinding of white or black peppercorns. Serve immediately.
Serves 4

fat-free

poached pineapple in red honey syrup, rose hips sorbet

Rose hips are the seed pods of the rose bush, once used primarily for making jelly. They impart a beautiful crimson to this honeyed poaching liquid, and contain an impressive amount of vitamin C. The dessert itself is both gastronomically and visually electrifying.

1 medium-large ripe **pineapple**

⅓ cup plus 2 teaspoons aromatic **honey**

4 **rose hips tea bags** (see Note) or 3 tablespoons dried rose hips

Using a very sharp knife, cut off the pineapple's crown along with the top inch of pineapple flesh. Then cut off the bottom ½ inch. Stand the pineapple upright and carefully cut down the sides, following the contour of the pineapple, until all the peel is removed. Be sure you cut deep enough so that all the "eyes" and rough skin are removed. Save the green leaves from the crown for garnishing. Lay peeled pineapple on its side and cut it crosswise into 4 thick slices.

Place pineapple in a nonreactive skillet large enough to hold the slices in a single layer. Add 5 cups water and ⅓ cup honey. Bring to a boil. Add rose hips and lower heat so that poaching liquid simmers gently. Cover skillet and cook for 15 to 20 minutes, then turn pineapple over. Cook, covered, for 15 minutes longer, or until tender. Remove pineapple with a slotted spoon and place in a shallow casserole. Discard tea bags. (If using loose rose hips, strain liquid through a sieve.)

Over high heat, cook the remaining liquid until reduced to 3 cups. Pour 1 cup over pineapple slices. Let cool, then cover and refrigerate until ready to serve.

Chill remaining 2 cups liquid in small bowl until very cold. Process in ice-cream machine according to manufacturer's directions until a smooth sorbet results.

With an apple corer or small knife, remove center woody core from each pineapple slice. Place pineapple slice and some poaching liquid in 4 large shallow soup bowls. Top with a scoop of sorbet. Drizzle each serving with ½ teaspoon honey. Garnish with a pineapple leaf sticking out of sorbet. Serve immediately.
Serves 4

Note: You can substitute Red Zinger tea bags for a similar flavor.

red and white cherry soup with star anise, cherry ice

This is a turn-your-tongue-red summer treat of fruit ices afloat in a fruit soup. Each is a singular treat when served alone, and although they are rarely combined, I think the flavors of sweet cherries and star anise were just meant for each other. Cultivated cherries are descended from species native to western Asia; star anise has been a secret ingredient in Chinese medicine for centuries.

FOR THE SOUP

1½ pounds ripe fresh **cherries**: a mixture of dark red and Royal Anne (or other white variety)

3 tablespoons **sugar**

7 whole **star anise**

Wash cherries. Remove stems. Carefully cut in half and remove pits.

In a 4-quart pot, bring 2½ cups water and sugar to a boil. Add 5 whole star anise, 2 star anise broken into a few pieces, halved cherries, and ¼ teaspoon each whole black and white peppercorns. Cook over medium-high heat for 20 minutes.

Using a slotted spoon, transfer cherries to a bowl. Cook remaining liquid over high heat until reduced to 1½ cups. Remove star anise and peppercorns with slotted spoon and set aside. Pour liquid over cherries. Refrigerate for several hours, until very cold. Serve in chilled shallow soup bowls, adding a whole star anise to each. Top with a small scoop of cherry ices; or, if you prefer, garnish each with a red and white cherry with stems.
Serves 4

FOR THE CHERRY ICE

¼ cup **sugar**

¾ pound dark red **cherries**

In a small saucepan bring 1¼ cups water and ¼ cup sugar to a boil. Boil for 2 minutes. Let cool.

Remove pits from ¾ pound cherries. Place in bowl of a food processor. Puree until very smooth.

Add cooled sugar syrup. Process until smooth.

Transfer to a shallow metal dish. Freeze for 3 hours, scraping with a fork every 30 minutes to break up ice crystals. Process briefly in food processor just before serving.
Serves 8

strawberry-ginger sorbet, macerated berries and ginger chips

Here's a wonderful example of using two ingredients two different ways. Ripe strawberries are lightly macerated with a bit of sugar and left to "stew in their own juices." More strawberries are pureed with fresh ginger and churned into a sorbet. More ginger is then sliced and baked into pungent, brittle chips.

2 pounds ripe **strawberries**

4-inch piece fresh **ginger**

7 tablespoons **sugar**

Wash berries and dry. Remove stems.

Place ¾ pound berries in bowl of a food processor. Place remaining berries in refrigerator and save for later. Peel ginger and finely chop a 1-inch piece. Add to food processor with a pinch of kosher salt and puree until very smooth. Place in a small bowl.

In a small saucepan, boil ¼ cup water and 3 tablespoons sugar for 1 minute, stirring until the sugar dissolves. Add the sugar mixture to the strawberry-ginger puree and chill until very cold. Freeze strawberry-ginger puree in an ice-cream machine according to manufacturer's directions.

Meanwhile, preheat oven to 250°F. Slice remaining ginger into long paper-thin slices. Toss with ½ tablespoon sugar. Place on parchment-lined baking sheet and bake for 1 hour, or until crisp, turning after 30 minutes. Remove from oven and sprinkle lightly with ½ teaspoon sugar. Let cool. These will stay crisp for about 24 hours.

Thirty to 60 minutes before serving, cut remaining berries (1¼ pounds) in half and place in a bowl. Add 3 tablespoons sugar and mix gently. Let sit at room temperature for 30 to 60 minutes.

When ready to serve, place berries and juices in dessert dishes or wine glasses; top with scoops of sorbet, and ginger chips stuck into sorbet. Serve immediately.

Serves 4

frosted lemons with yogurt gelato

This lemon-yogurt blend is a cooling zephyr for the entire body. Serve these little frozen treats on unsprayed fresh lemon leaves.

11 large **lemons**

⅞ cup superfine **sugar**

1½ cups **low-fat plain yogurt**

Grate the rind of 3 lemons to yield 1 tablespoon grated zest. Squeeze these lemons and 1 or 2 more to yield ¾ cup juice. Reserve 6 lemons.

In a large nonreactive bowl, whisk together lemon juice, zest, sugar, and a pinch of salt. Stir until sugar dissolves. Whisk in yogurt and blend thoroughly. Chill until very cold.

Cut ⅓-inch oval slice off one side of each of 6 reserved lemons (to resemble a little canoe), saving these "hats." Cut out most of the pulp with a paring knife and then, with a spoon, scrape the remaining pulp from the sides and discard pulp. Turn the lemons cut side down on paper towels to drain.

Pour chilled yogurt mixture into an ice-cream machine and freeze according to manufacturer's directions.

Cut small slices from top of inverted lemons so they sit firmly when turned over. Fill each lemon with yogurt gelato, mounding high over the shell, and top with the lemon "hat." Freeze until hard. Let sit for 10 to 15 minutes, at room temperature, before serving.

Serves 6

baked plums with walnut crunch, red plum sauce

When served slightly warm, ripe, voluptuous plums burst with juices. Round and red Santa Rosas are perfect for this dish. A rich filling of aromatic cinnamon-sugar and walnuts replaces the pits.

8 large, firm red **plums**

3 ounces shelled **walnuts**

3½ tablespoons **cinnamon-sugar** (page 14) or store-bought

Preheat oven to 400°F.

Wash plums. Cut in half and remove pits.

Place walnuts in bowl of a food processor with 2 tablespoons cinnamon-sugar. Process until finely ground. Add 2 tablespoons water and process briefly until a paste is formed.

Place nut paste in cavities of 12 plum halves only. Sprinkle each with a little cinnamon sugar, using up to 1 tablespoon.

Place filled and unfilled plums on a baking sheet. Bake for 10 minutes and place briefly under the broiler so that nut mixture is golden. Using a spatula, transfer filled plums to a platter. Let cool.

Place unfilled plums in bowl of food processor with ¼ cup water and ½ tablespoon cinnamon-sugar. Process until very smooth. Let cool.

When ready to serve, divide plum sauce among dessert plates. Top with 2 filled plum halves per plate.

Serves 6

orange gratin with pineapple-orange sabayon

This sunny and sophisticated dessert, sweetened with reduced pineapple juice, is high in calcium, potassium, and vitamin C. Serving it warm accentuates its flavor, aroma, and drama.

7 large juice **oranges**

½ cup unsweetened **pineapple juice**

4 large **egg yolks**

Wash oranges and dry well. Grate rind of 2 oranges to yield 2 teaspoons grated zest. Set aside.

Peel and segment 6 oranges: Using a small sharp knife, cut off the 2 polar ends of each orange. Cut down the sides of the oranges to remove all peel and white pith. Gently cut along the side of each segment, right next to the membrane, and out again at the next membrane, releasing segment but leaving membrane behind. Drain segments well. (If desired, retain some rind for garnish. Remove white pith and cut rind into fine julienne strips. Boil 5 minutes. Drain and set aside.)

In the centers of 4 large heat-proof plates, place orange segments, touching one another, in a tight pinwheel pattern. Cover with plastic wrap and refrigerate until ready to use.

Cut remaining orange in half and squeeze ¼ cup juice. Set juice aside.

Place pineapple juice in a small nonreactive saucepan and, over medium-high heat, cook until reduced by slightly more than half, to 3 tablespoons. Let cool.

In a double boiler or in a nonreactive bowl set over simmering water, whisk together grated zest,

orange juice, reduced pineapple juice, and egg yolks. Whisk continuously for 10 to 15 minutes over simmering water, until the mixture is thick and its volume has increased substantially. Make sure, while you are whisking, that the mixture does not get too hot, or the sabayon will curdle. From time to time, lift the top of the double boiler (or bowl) up and away from the lower pot containing the simmering water for a few seconds so that the mixture does not overheat. The finished consistency should be like soft whipped cream. Remove from heat.

Preheat broiler.

Remove plates with arranged orange segments from refrigerator. Discard plastic wrap. Lightly and gently blot each plate and orange arrangement with a paper towel. Using a spatula, gently swirl a thick layer of sabayon evenly over the oranges. Place under broiler, about 6 inches away, for about 15 to 30 seconds, just until sabayon begins to take on a golden color. Watch carefully; do not walk away. You can do this in several batches. Let cool for 10 minutes if serving warm. Or serve at room temperature within 2 hours. Garnish with reserved julienned orange rind, if desired.

Serves 4

warm rhubarb compote, vanilla yogurt timbale

Related to buckwheat, rhubarb is, botanically speaking, not a fruit but rather an herbaceous plant. While its leaves are deadly, its dark pink stems are high in calcium and potassium. They are exquisitely tart, so I've cooked them with red currant jelly for a delicious warm compote to accompany a slow-melting timbale of half-frozen vanilla yogurt.

2 cups **low-fat vanilla yogurt**

1½ pounds fresh **rhubarb**

½ cup best-quality **currant jelly**

Evenly spoon yogurt into six 3-ounce paper cups. Place in freezer for about 1 hour, until semifrozen. Preheat oven to 400°F.

Remove any green leaves from rhubarb and discard (they are poisonous). Cut rhubarb into 1½- to 2-inch lengths on the bias. Wash in colander. Drain, but do not dry.

Place rhubarb in a shallow casserole. Add jelly.

Stir until all pieces are coated.

Bake for 35 minutes, until rhubarb is tender, stirring twice during baking. Remove from oven.

Let compote cool for 5 minutes. Divide warm compote among 6 shallow soup bowls or glass coupes. Unmold yogurt cups and place next to or on top of rhubarb. Serve immediately.
Serves 6

cider-poached apples, cider syrup and swirls of cream

There's a Dutch still-life quality to this stunning dessert, for in a computer age in which everything's hyper-real, these apples are slumped, wrinkled, and moody. But, oh, the flavor, accentuated with a syrup made of apple cider. Researchers at Yale say that just sniffing apples can calm you down; so, I think, can looking at these.

4 medium-large red **apples** (your favorite variety)

2½ cups **apple cider**

3 tablespoons **heavy cream**

Wash apples. Cut in half, lengthwise, through the stem end. Using a melon baller, cut out area with seeds, making a perfect round hole. In a large pot with cover, put apple halves, cider, and 2 cups water, or enough to cover. Bring to a boil. Cover pot, lower heat to medium, and cook for 20 to 25 minutes, until apples are tender but not falling apart. Remove with a slotted spoon and let cool on a platter.

Increase heat under pot and bring liquid to a boil. Lower heat to medium and cook for about 20 minutes, until liquid is reduced to a thick syrup, about ½ cup. Let cool for 5 to 10 minutes.

Whip cream in a chilled bowl using a balloon whip. Whip until just thickened, but still a little runny.

Place 1 apple half in each of 4 shallow soup bowls or dessert plates. Cut other half into 2 wedges and place next to apple half. Spoon some whipped cream over apples and spoon warm syrup over cream and apples. Optional: Garnish with apple chips (below) if desired.

To make apple chips: Preheat oven to 250°F. Slice 1 additional apple very thin. Place on parchment-lined baking sheet. Bake for 1 hour, turning after 30 minutes. Turn again after 1 hour, then turn off oven but leave in oven to crisp for about 1 hour.

Serves 4

french walnut torte

It's nearly impossible to create a cake with three ingredients, but here's one—ethereally light and good for you, too. Finely ground walnuts take the place of flour, and the rest is based on careful technique. Walnuts may not cure your migraine, as the ancient Greeks believed, but they provide omega-3 fatty acids.

6 ounces best-quality shelled **walnuts**

6 large **egg whites** and 4 **egg yolks**

⅔ cup plus 1½ tablespoons **sugar**

Preheat oven to 350°F. Coat an 8½-inch spring-form pan with nonstick vegetable spray. Line bottom of pan with a round of parchment or waxed paper. Then coat paper liner with vegetable spray.

Lightly toast walnuts in a nonstick skillet over low heat. Allow to cool. In a food processor fitted with steel blade, process with 1 tablespoon sugar until finely ground.

Separate egg whites from yolks while eggs are cold from the refrigerator. Then allow them to come to room temperature.

In bowl of an electric mixer, beat whites with a pinch of salt on medium speed until white and frothy. Gradually increase speed to high and beat until stiff but not dry. Do not overbeat.

In another large bowl, using electric mixer, combine egg yolks and 3 tablespoons water. Beat on medium speed and gradually add ⅔ cup sugar. Increase speed to medium-high and continue beating until yolk mixture is thick and pale yellow. Using a rubber spatula, stir in nuts until just combined. Gently fold beaten whites into batter, deflating whites as little as possible.

Pour batter into prepared pan. Level top of batter with a spatula and sprinkle with remaining ½ tablespoon sugar.

Bake for 45 minutes. Do not open oven door during baking.

Remove from oven. Transfer to a rack and allow to cool completely. Cake will settle as it cools. When completely cool, run a small, thin-bladed knife between side of pan and cake. Open springform and remove side of pan from cake.

Serves 12

cocoa meringues

This is the cookie that could launch a thousand milk moustaches. Five of these cocoa puffs have only 90 calories and no fat. Nutritional experts know that cocoa contains flavonoids, protective phytochemicals that keep our cells healthy. Food experts and moms know that cookies go with milk.

6 large **egg whites**

6 tablespoons good-quality unsweetened **cocoa powder**

6 tablespoons **sugar**

Preheat oven to 250°F.

In bowl of electric mixer, beat egg whites with a pinch of salt until they form soft peaks. Mix cocoa and sugar together and slowly add to whites. Beat until stiff peaks form.

Place a piece of parchment paper on a baking sheet. Drop heaping 1½ tablespoons of batter on sheet to make each cookie. Bake for 1 hour. Remove from oven and let cool on sheet.

Makes 26 cookies

chocolate mousse sponge

This is a perfect dessert when only real chocolate will do—a small slice will satisfy the most decadent of cravings. You can have your cake and drink it, too, by serving this with a glass of red wine and a cup of black tea. They all contain flavonoids—specific antioxidants that may protect against heart disease and certain cancers. Use the darkest chocolate possible for the greatest benefit and deepest flavor.

8 ounces best-quality **semisweet chocolate** (such as Callebaut or Valrhona)

8 large **eggs**

¼ cup **confectioners' sugar** plus 2 tablespoons for dusting

Preheat oven to 350°F. Lightly coat sides of an 8½-inch springform pan with nonstick vegetable spray and line bottom with waxed paper.

Melt chocolate in a double boiler or in a metal bowl set over a saucepan of simmering water, stirring until smooth. Remove from heat and keep chocolate warm over the water.

Separate egg whites from yolks while eggs are cold from the refrigerator. Then allow them to come to room temperature. Whisk yolks until thick and pale yellow, about 2 minutes with a standing mixer or 4 minutes with a hand-held. (Do not beat to ribbon stage.) Fold chocolate into yolks.

Using thoroughly cleaned beaters, beat whites with ¼ cup sugar and a pinch of salt, until they just hold soft peaks. Fold one-fourth of whites into

chocolate mixture to lighten, then fold in remaining whites gently but thoroughly.

Pour batter into pan and bake in middle of oven, 25 to 30 minutes, just until cake is almost set but still trembles slightly in center when shaken gently. Do not cook it beyond this stage, or you won't get a mousselike center. Cool cake on a rack (it will settle as it cools) and chill (still in pan), covered, at least 6 hours.

Let cake stand at room temperature for 30 minutes before serving. Run a small, thin-bladed knife between side of pan and cake. Open springform and remove side of pan from cake. Dust with confectioners sugar.

Serves 12

a simple vanilla gâteau

Somewhere between a sponge and an angel (-food cake, that is), this low-fat dessert seems to levitate magically and then holds its shape.

6 large **egg whites** and 4 **egg yolks**

1¼ cups plus 2 teaspoons **vanilla sugar** (page 15) or store-bought

1⅓ cups **self-rising cake flour**

Preheat oven to 350°F. Coat a 9-inch springform pan with nonstick vegetable spray. Line bottom of pan with a round of parchment or waxed paper. Then coat paper liner with the vegetable spray.

Separate egg whites from yolks while eggs are cold from the refrigerator. Then allow them to come to room temperature.

In bowl of an electric mixer, beat egg whites together with a pinch of salt on medium speed until white and frothy. Gradually add ¼ cup sugar. Increase speed to high and beat until stiff and glossy but not dry. Do not overbeat.

In another bowl, using electric mixer, combine egg yolks with 3 tablespoons water. Beat on medium speed and gradually add 1 cup sugar. Increase speed to medium-high and continue beating until yolk mixture is thick and pale yellow. Sift flour onto yolk mixture and use a large rubber spatula to gently and thoroughly combine. Mixture will be stiff.

Add about one-quarter of the beaten whites to the yolk mixture and gently mix until just combined. Empty bowl with yolk mixture into bowl with remaining whites. Using a large rubber spatula, gently fold until just combined, deflating mixture as little as possible.

Pour batter into prepared pan, smoothing the top with a spatula. Sprinkle with remaining 2 teaspoons sugar.

Bake for 35 minutes. Remove from oven. Transfer to a rack and allow to cool completely. When completely cool, run a small, thin-bladed knife between side of pan and cake. Open springform and remove side of pan from cake.

Serves 8

cinnamon-chocolate ciambella

Ciambella is an Italian name for a traditional ring-shaped cake and is the inspiration for this pretty treat. Cinnamon adds depth to the flavor of cocoa, a defatted and powdered form of chocolate. Many people use both to dust their cappuccino, which probably is redundant with a slice of this cake.

8 large **eggs**

⅔ cup **cinnamon-sugar** plus 1 tablespoon (page 14) or store-bought

⅓ cup plus 1 tablespoon good-quality Dutch-process **cocoa**

Preheat oven to 375°F. Thoroughly spray a 10-inch Bundt pan with nonstick vegetable spray.

Separate egg whites from yolks while eggs are cold from the refrigerator. Then allow them to come to room temperature.

In bowl of an electric mixer, beat whites with a pinch of salt on medium speed until frothy. Gradually add ⅓ cup cinnamon-sugar. Increase speed to high and beat until stiff and glossy but not dry. Do not overbeat.

In another bowl, using electric mixer, combine egg yolks with 1 tablespoon water. Beat on medium speed and gradually add ⅓ cup cinnamon-sugar. Increase speed to medium-high and continue beating until yolk mixture is thick and pale yellow. Place ⅓ cup cocoa in a sifter or a sieve and sift onto yolk mixture. Using a large rubber spatula, gently and thoroughly combine cocoa with yolk mixture.

Add about one-quarter of the beaten whites to the yolk mixture and gently mix until just combined. Empty bowl with yolk mixture into bowl with remaining whites. Using a large rubber spatula, gently fold until just combined, deflating mixture as little as possible.

Pour batter into prepared pan. Tap firmly against counter to release air bubbles.

Bake for 28 to 30 minutes. Remove from oven. Transfer to rack and allow to cool completely. Cake will deflate dramatically. When completely cool, run a thin metal skewer (or narrow knife) around the circumference of the inner core of the Bundt pan. Place a serving plate over the pan and, holding the pan and dish together, invert. Bundt pan should now be upside down on serving dish. Carefully and gently lift pan straight up, releasing cake onto serving dish. Sift remaining 1 tablespoon cocoa onto top of cake.

Serves 8

cinnamon-sugar crisps

These elegant wafers are made from wonton skins sprinkled with aromatic cinnamon-sugar. A bit of butter adds a lot of rich flavor.

32 **wonton wrappers** (see Note)

2 tablespoons unsalted **butter**, melted

2½ tablespoons **cinnamon-sugar** (page 14) or store-bought

Preheat oven to 400°F.

Place wonton wrappers on baking sheets. Brush evenly with melted butter. Sprinkle evenly with cinnamon-sugar.

Bake for 5 minutes, or until crisp. Cool on wire racks.

Makes 32 crisps

Note: Wonton wrappers (or "skins") are available in small packages in the refrigerated section of Asian and specialty food stores and most supermarkets.

biscottini

Twice-baked, doubly delicious. Good for dunking, great for dieting with only 1 gram of fat per cookie.

2 large **eggs**

⅔ cup **vanilla sugar** or cinnamon-sugar (pages 14 and 15) or store-bought

1 cup all-purpose **flour**

Preheat oven to 400°F.

Coat an 8½-by-4½-by-2½-inch nonstick loaf pan with vegetable spray.

Place eggs in bowl of an electric mixer with a pinch of salt. Beat on medium-high speed until eggs are very thick, 5 to 6 minutes. Gradually add the cinnamon-sugar and beat for 1 minute longer.

Using a coarse-mesh sieve, sift flour over egg mixture. With a large rubber spatula, fold flour into egg mixture gently and thoroughly.

Pour batter evenly into prepared pan. Smooth top with spatula.

Bake until firm to the touch, 25 to 30 minutes. Remove from oven and let cool in pan on rack for 15 minutes.

Lower oven temperature to 275°F.

Line a large baking sheet with parchment paper.

Carefully run a thin-bladed knife around sides of pan and remove loaf from pan. With a serrated knife, using a gentle sawing motion, slice into 18 to 20 ¼-inch-thick slices on a slight bias. Place slices on prepared baking sheet. Bake for 8 minutes. Carefully turn slices over and bake for another 8 minutes.

Let cool on a wire rack. Store in an air-tight container.

Makes 18 to 20 biscottini

For those who don't covet sweets but are passionate about cheese after their meal, here are some delightful combinations, in tandem with fruit. The pairings have been designed for optimal contrast of flavor and texture: sweet fruit with salty cheese; creamy cheese with crisp fruit; pungent with floral; juicy with crumbly, and so on.

Some rules to follow: The more flavorful the cheese, the more satisfying the experience. So forget low-fat, packaged products. Younger cheeses are more delicate; older cheeses are more concentrated and sometimes more pungent. It is interesting to try them side by side. All of these cheeses are best at room temperature (so think ahead).

low calorie

cabrales cheese with roasted grapes

½ pound each: red and green seedless **grapes**

8 ounces **Cabrales cheese**, chilled

8 teaspoons aromatic **honey**

Preheat oven to 275°F.

Wash grapes and pat dry. Cut grapes into small clusters, the size of a small apple. Place grape clusters on a baking sheet and place in oven. Bake for 1½ hours, turning once or twice, until grapes have lost much of their moisture and have slightly caramelized. Clusters will retain their shape. Remove from oven and let cool just to room temperature but not cold.

Cut cheese into 8 equal slices. Put a slice of cheese in center of each of 8 large plates and let come to room temperature.

Place small clumps of grapes, using both red and green, on each slice of cheese. Drizzle with 1 teaspoon honey. Serve with a fork and knife. *Serves 8*

low calorie

brie and seckel pear, dried figs

4 ounces ripe **Brie** at room temperature

4 ripe **seckel pears**

4 **dried figs**

Cut cheese into 4 equal slices. Wash pears and dry thoroughly. Cut in half lengthwise. Cut halves into long thin wedges. Arrange next to cheese. Cut figs in half and place two halves on each plate. *Serves 4*

cantaloupe with manchego and honey

½ small ripe **cantaloupe**

3-ounce piece **Manchego cheese**

4 teaspoons aromatic **honey**

Remove rind from melon and discard seeds.

Cut melon into paper-thin wedges. Each portion should be about 4 thin slices. Arrange on plate. Drizzle 1 teaspoon honey over each serving. Slice cheese into thin slivers and scatter over melon. Sprinkle with coarsely ground black pepper.
Serves 4

watermelon, feta, and mint

1¼-pound wedge of ripe red or yellow **watermelon**

5 ounces **feta cheese**, in one piece

1 small bunch **mint**

Remove rind and seeds from melon. Carefully cut into ¼-inch cubes. Place in a bowl. Wash mint and dry thoroughly. Cut mint into fine julienne, saving some whole leaves for garnish. Add about 6 table-spoons julienned mint to melon and gently mix. Let sit 5 minutes.

Mound melon in center of 4 large plates. Thinly slice cheese and arrange next to melon, or crumble cheese and scatter on top. Garnish with a few whole mint leaves, or more julienned mint.
Serves 4

bosc pears and parmigiano-reggiano, melon liqueur

2 large ripe **Bosc pears**

1½ tablespoons **melon liqueur** (such as Midori)

2 ounces **Parmigiano-Reggiano**, in one piece

Peel pears. Cut in half lengthwise and remove seeds. Cut through the width on the bias to make ¼-inch-thick pieces. Place in a bowl and add melon liqueur. Toss to coat thoroughly and let sit for 5 minutes.

Place sliced pears on serving plates. Cut cheese into thin slices and scatter over pears.
Serves 4

stilton cheese with roasted lady apples, port syrup

¾ cup **ruby port**

4 **lady apples** with stems, 2 ounces each

3 ounces **Stilton cheese**

Put port in a small saucepan and bring to a boil. Lower heat to medium and cook for 10 to 15 minutes, or until reduced to ¼ cup. Let cool.

Preheat oven to 450°F. Wash apples and place in a pie tin. Roast for 20 minutes. Remove from oven. Let cool for 10 minutes.

Remove any waxy rind from cheese. Cut into 4 slices. Place flat on plates. Drizzle with port syrup. Place apple next to cheese.
Serves 4

healthy menus with wine

A savvy statistician could calculate the staggering number of menus that can be assembled from this book's 200 plus recipes, but I've compiled here 32 sumptuous menus with three or more courses that respect my 1-2-3 dietary objectives.

1. Menus **very low in fat** contain 1 to 5 grams of fat and fewer than 675 calories;

2. Menus **very low in calories** contain fewer than 500 calories, with fewer than 30 percent of their calories from fat; and

3. Menus that are **low fat and low cal** have 650 to 750 calories, with 30 percent or fewer of their calories from fat.

Included are "grapenotes": my wine recommendations for each healthy menu. After all, medical experts tell us that wine can be an integral part of a balanced diet. Although white wines and red often will cozy up to a meal equally well, my choices, when appropriate, lean toward reds in order to derive the health benefits described in the introduction (page 13). Their range is appealing—from Sangiovese from California to new Cabernet Franc from Argentina, robust Shiraz from Australia to delicately perfumed Pinot Noir from Oregon.

Calorically, a 5-ounce glass of dry wine (whether red, white, or rosé) adds about 110 to 120 calories to a meal. Most of those calories are in the alcohol, so when you cook with wine and evaporate the alcohol, wine leaves only its incomparable flavor. A glass of sweet wine to accompany dessert (or sometimes instead of dessert) is 45 calories an ounce. A little goes a long way, as a 3- or 3½-ounce pour adds 135 to 157 calories. Champagne flutes hold about 3½ ounces and a glass of brut contains about 84 calories.

Aside from the nutritional aspects of wine, these are a few things to consider gastronomically when choosing wines: Acidity in wine leaves your palate feeling refreshed and clean. A bit of sweetness in wine can offset salty or spicy flavors in food. Oaky wines partner well with full-bodied dishes. Sweet food will overpower dry wine. Acidic wines can mirror the tartness in food. You could spend a lifetime discovering the many pleasures of thoughtfully pairing wine and food. I suggest keeping a diary of wine and food combinations that have especially pleased you and your guests so you can replicate the experience.

À votre santé! To your health!

Healthy Menus

very low fat

1 to 5 grams of fat
Under 675 calories

	Cal	Fat
"Penicillin" (in a demitasse cup)	40	<1
Assiette of Fall Vegetables:		
Tiny Lentils with Port-Glazed Shallots	273	0
Raspberry-Kissed Red Cabbage	97	0
Brussels Sprouts with		
Orange-Balsamic Reduction	108	0
Anjou Pears and Grappa	152	0
Total	670	<1
	<1% calories from fat	

Grapenote: A bottle of Beaujolais-Villages will integrate the flavors of this simple menu with style.

	Cal	Fat
Jumbo Shrimp on the Half Shell,		
"8-Vegetable" Granita	34	2
Turkey Salad with Grape Tomatoes		
and Zucchini, Zucchini Coulis	230	1
Grated Carrot–Citrus Salad	49	0
Mangoes and Blackberries,		
Blackberry Coulis	215	0
Total	628	3
	4% calories from fat	

Grapenote: Enjoy an unusual, affordable dry vinho verde from Portugal or a weightier Spanish white like Godello.

	Cal	Fat
Thick Fennel Soup with Spinach Pastina	105	1
Lemon Sole in Tomato		
and Preserved Lemon Sauce	286	3
Green Vegetables à la Vapeur	60	0
Rosemary-Poached Pears "Vino Cotto"	218	0
Total	669	4
	5% calories from fat	

Grapenote: This menu requires a white wine with character. Try a Greco di Tufo from the south of Italy or a lusty white from Sicily.

	Cal	Fat
Steamed Mussels al Finocchio,		
Toasted Fennel Fronds (half portion)	172	2
Whole-Wheat Linguine		
in the Style of Sardinia (half portion)	154	2
Broccoli di Rape with Sultanas	119	0
Melon au Porto	155	0
Total	600	4
	6% calories from fat	

Grapenote: Something crisp, dry, and Italian would be perfect here: Verdicchio or pinot grigio. Or a light red Bardolino, slightly chilled.

	Cal	Fat
Chilled Oysters, Sake-Shallot Mignonette	133	2
Chilled Spring Pea Soup	144	2
with Lemon-Poppy Wafer	30	1
Jicama with Lime and Cilantro	73	0
Crown of Green Figs and Raspberries,		
Rock Sugar and Fig Coulis	288	0
Total	668	5
	7% calories from fat	

Grapenote: A dry rosé champagne would be just the thing, beginning to end.

	Cal	Fat
Zucchini Foam with Crab	81	1
Rolled and Tied Turkey Roast with Fresh		
Sage and Baked Pears (without skin)	278	3
Red Chard with Garlic Cream	70	1
My Favorite Sweet Potatoes	191	0
Cherry Ice	49	0
Total	669	5
	7% calories from fat	

Grapenote: Open a luscious Pinot Noir from Oregon, Washington State, or California's central coast.

very low calorie

Under 500 calories
10 to 16 grams of fat/30% and under calories from fat

	Cal	Fat
Cauliflower Vichyssoise with Chive Cream	73	4
Sautéed Shrimp in Corn-Milk Sauce	165	6
Summer Squash with Fresh Basil	73	5
Strawberry-Ginger Sorbet,		
Macerated Berries and Ginger Chips	<u>165</u>	<u>0</u>
Total	476	15
	28% calories from fat	

Grapenote: A soft, earthy varietal such as Viognier, from California or France, your choice.

	Cal	Fat
Zucchini Foam with Crab	81	1
Poached Salmon, Cilantro-Yogurt Sauce	165	6
Lemon-Poppy Wafer	30	1
Grated Carrot–Citrus Salad	49	0
Fresh Blueberries and		
Blueberry Compote, Lemon "Custard"	<u>165</u>	<u>2</u>
Total	490	10
	18% calories from fat	

Grapenote: How about a white wine with lots of character and flavor? A Sauvignon Blanc from South Africa or Vidal Blanc from Rhode Island.

	Cal	Fat
Garlic Soup with Chicken and Cilantro	114	1
Sautéed Cod with Asparagus,		
Asparagus Velouté	261	10
Yellow Tomato Salsa	39	0
"Canary" Soup with Melon Balls,		
Mint, and Lime Oil	<u>80</u>	<u>≤1</u>
Total	494	12
	22% calories from fat	

Grapenote: A well-respected Fumé Blanc from California would be a mouthwatering match.

	Cal	Fat
Broccoli Soup with Fresh Basil Butter	90	6
Baked Fennel Parmigiana (half portion)	135	4
Polenta Tart with Melted Tomatoes		
and Smoked Mozzarella (half portion)	145	4
Poached Pineapple in Red Honey Syrup	<u>114</u>	<u>0</u>
Total	484	14
	26% calories from fat	

Grapenote: This menu demands some acidity and fruit, so go with a Barbera from Italy. For white-wine lovers, open an un-oaked Chardonnay from Australia, instead.

	Cal	Fat
1-2-3 Tomato Salad		
with Ricotta Salata and Dill	128	5
Parmesan-Crusted Asparagus, Poached Egg	165	9
Red Chard with Garlic Cream	70	1
Macerated Strawberries with Ginger Chips	87	0
Cocoa Meringue	<u>18</u>	<u>0</u>
Total	468	15
	29% calories from fat	

Grapenote: You will want a stylish Italian dry rosé, a chiaretto or a rosato, or a graceful rosé from France.

	Cal	Fat
Jean-Georges' Leek Terrine with Caviar	214	5
Seared Smoked Salmon, Cucumbers		
Pressé	149	9
1-2-3 Fruit Soup	<u>116</u>	<u>0</u>
Total	479	14
	26% calories from fat	

Grapenote: This requires something with bubbles and austerity to cut through all the richness. Pop the cork of a good California sparkler.

	Cal	Fat
Honeydew "Carpaccio" with Air-Dried Beef		
and Asiago	152	5
Polenta with Gorgonzola and Peas	189	5
Red and White Cherry Soup with Star Anise	<u>138</u>	<u>0</u>
Total	479	10
	19% calories from fat	

Grapenote: Some Prosecco for the first course, then a glass of red with some depth for the second course: a Sangiovese from California or Chianti Classico from Italy.

low fat and low calorie

10 to 25 grams of fat,
650 to 750 calories/30% and under calories from fat

	Cal	Fat
Steamed Asparagus with Wasabi Butter	105	8
Pepper-Seared Mahi Mahi, Mango Salsa	315	9
Yucca Puree with Buttermilk and Chives	165	1
Iced Green Tea with Lemongrass Infusion	35	0
Strawberry-Ginger Sorbet (half-portion)	39	0
Total	659	18
	25% calories from fat	

Grapenote: Open a big, fruity but dry Riesling from Oregon or California. An off-dry Vouvray from the Loire Valley also will be satisfying.

	Cal	Fat
Roasted Tomato–Pepper Gazpacho, Basil Oil	141	9
Parmesan Crisp	35	1
Seared Swordfish with Fresh Corn,		
Chipotle "Cream"	331	9
Poached Seckel Pears,		
Maple-Cardamom Syrup	165	0
Total	672	19
	25% calories from fat	

Grapenote: A sturdy sem-chard from Australia with a touch of sweetness would be special. Or go in a different direction with a white Côtes du Rhône with lots of Viognier.

	Cal	Fat
Chilled Spring Pea Soup	144	2
Salmon Arrosto with Rosemary	320	13
Petite Ratatouille	64	4
Frosted Lemon with Yogurt Gelato	151	1
Total	679	20
	27% calories from fat	

Grapenote: Here's a chance to do red wine with fish; try a fairly light Washington State Pinot Noir.

	Cal	Fat
Chilled Oysters, Sake-Shallot Mignonette	133	2
Lacquered Salmon, Pineapple-Soy Reduction	318	10
Julienned Snow Peas with		
Lemon Oil and Poppy Seeds	91	5
Rose Hips Sorbet	90	0
Cinnamon-Sugar Crisp	33	1
Total	665	18
	24% calories from fat	

Grapenote: These distinctive flavors will segue into each other with a dry Gewürztraminer from Alsace.

	Cal	Fat
Warm Roasted Beets,		
Balsamic Syrup and Crispy Greens	150	0
Penne with Zucchini, Zucchini-Garlic Sauce	350	15
Little Tomato-Pesto "Napoleons"	105	5
Pear Granita	83	0
Total	688	20
	26% calories from fat	

Grapenote: Try one of Italy's exciting new varietals, like Chardonnay from a great producer.

	Cal	Fat
Iced Cucumber-Spearmint Soup	86	2
Cumin-Crusted Lamb with Apricots	346	11
Persian Rice with Saffron Broth	157	3
Grated Carrot–Citrus Salad	49	0
Rose Hips Sorbet	90	0
Total	728	16
	20% calories from fat	

Grapenote: A supple, well-rounded Merlot, from California or the south of France, is a lovely match. So is a more geographically correct red from Lebanon or Israel.

	Cal	Fat
Poached Leeks with Roasted Garlic		
and Brie Fondue	165	8
Layered Flounder and Smoked Salmon	333	6
Green Vegetables à la Vapeur	60	0
Pineapple Shingles with Caramel,		
Pistachio Dust	165	4
Total	723	18
	22% calories from fat	

Grapenote: This meal calls for a big, fat, mouth-filling Chardonnay from California, one with evident oak.

	Cal	Fat
Plum Tomato Salad with Bocconcini		
and Tomato Frappé	130	7
Orecchiette with Broccoli,		
Broccoli-Butter Sauce	350	9
Celery Gratinée with Prosciutto	97	6
Frosted Lemon with Yogurt Gelato	151	1
Total	728	23
	28% calories from fat	

Grapenote: This menu is a trip to Italy, so select a lighter-style Chianti or heavy-duty white from one of your favorite regions.

	Cal	Fat
A Trio of Roasted Peppers and		
Radish Sprouts, Creamy Feta Dressing	100	4
Red Hens with Sumac and Shallots	324	15
Persian Rice with Saffron Broth	157	3
Red Chard with Garlic Cream	70	1
"Canary" Soup with Melon Balls,		
Mint and Lime Oil	80	0
Total	731	23
	28% calories from fat	

Grapenote: Go for red—something luscious but light, with ripe fruit flavors, like a big Beaujolais or a Cabernet Franc.

	Cal	Fat
Yellow Split Pea and		
Smoked Salmon Bisque	261	2
Sauteed Cod with Asparagus,		
Asparagus Velouté	261	10
Sugar Snaps and Sweet Pepper		
Julienne, Red Pepper Sauce	100	7
Poached Pineapple in Red Honey Syrup	114	0
Total	736	19
	23% calories from fat	

Grapenote: Sophisticated choices would include a dry Riesling from Alsace, or a Seyval Blanc from New York State.

	Cal	Fat
Wasabi Clams with Pickled Ginger	119	1
Poached Salmon, Cilantro-Yogurt Sauce	165	6
Five-Minute Corn with Aged Tamari	165	6
Julienned Beefsteak Tomato Salad,		
Watercress Oil	149	11
Red and White Cherry Soup		
with Star Anise	138	0
Total	736	24
	29% calories from fat	

Grapenote: For this summery menu, try a dry, complex rosé from the south of France or a mouthwatering blush from the Navarre province of Spain.

	Cal	Fat
A Trio of Roasted Peppers with		
Radish Sprouts, Creamy Feta Dressing	100	4
Tandoori Chicken on the Bone	335	6
Minted Couscous with Curry Oil	194	5
Fresh Apricots in Cinnamon Syrup	115	0
Total	744	15
	18% calories from fat	

Grapenote: This style of food demands a spicy, forward, medium-bodied mate: German Riesling with a nuance of sweetness would be interesting.

	Cal	Fat
Jicama with Lime and Cilantro	73	0
Brined Pork Loin with Orange-Chipotle Jus	330	12
Buckwheat Groats		
with "Caramelized" Onions	151	1
Steamed Mustard Greens,		
Roasted Garlic Butter	115	7
Cocoa Meringues (4 per serving)	72	0
Total	741	20
	24% calories from fat	

Grapenote: No wimpy wines need apply here! Go for a good Shiraz from South Africa or Australia.

	Cal	Fat
Endive Leaves and "Endive Marmalade,"		
White Balsamic Vinaigrette	137	11
Duck Magret with Roasted Red Onions		
and Pomegranate Molasses	350	12
Bulghur with Morels and Dried Cherries	195	0
Chocolate-Orange Sorbet	60	0
Total	742	23
	28% calories from fat	

Grapenote: This lucky duck deserves a good Rhône red—a Gigondas or a Châteauneuf-du-Pape.

	Cal	Fat
Cauliflower Vichyssoise with Chive Cream	73	4
Salmon Demi-Cuit, Sauce Moutarde	350	17
Scalloped Cheese Potatoes	165	4
Green Vegetables à la Vapeur	60	0
Almond Sorbetto	78	0
Cocoa Meringue	18	0
Total	744	25
	30% calories from fat	

Grapenote: Elegant menus deserve elegant wines, so go directly to Burgundy. Open a big white, a less-expensive but earthy Rully, or a suave red, the older the better.

	Cal	Fat
Jumbo Shrimp on the Half Shell,		
"8-Vegetable" Granita	134	2
Rib-Eye Roast, Gravlax-Style	349	18
Frenched String Beans		
with Sweet Garlic Sauce	79	5
Raspberry-Kissed Red Cabbage	97	0
Pear Granita	86	0
Total	745	25
30% calories from fat		

Grapenote: Break out a robust California Cabernet Sauvignon or a slightly softer Merlot. Buy the best you can afford.

	Cal	Fat
Zucchini Foam with Crab	81	1
Next Wave Tuna Salad: Tartare and Seared	346	16
Yellow Tomato Salsa	39	0
Radish Raita	77	2
Orange Gratin with		
Pineapple-Orange Sabayon	205	5
Total	748	24
29% calories from fat		

Grapenote: White or red wine will take this menu in two different, yet exciting directions. A spicy, medium-bodied dry Gewürztraminer from Alsace; or a light-style spicy Zinfandel from California can harmonize these vivid flavors.

	Cal	Fat
Wasabi Clams with Pickled Ginger	119	1
Cold Poached Chicken,		
Avocado and Mango Mousseline	346	12
Jicama with Lime and Cilantro	73	0
Pink Grapefruit in Guava Nectar,		
Candied Violets	212	0
Total	750	13
16% calories from fat		

Grapenote: Soon to be trendy, Grüner Veltliner from Austria goes with this East-West menu. It's snappy and floral, with delicate herbal undertones.

	Cal	Fat
Roasted Asparagus and Orange Salad,		
Asparagus "Fettuccine"	148	7
Bluefish under a Brick,		
Whole-Poached Scallions	284	9
My Favorite Sweet Potatoes	191	0
Peaches in Peach Schnapps with Basil	123	0
Total	746	16
19% calories from fat		

Grapenote: A white Bordeaux would be great: it will cut through the bluefish and not be wiped out by the asparagus or the ginger in the sweet potatoes.

fat and calorie index

SOUPS

	Cal	Fat
Broccoli Soup with Fresh Basil Butter	90	6
Caldo Verde: Potato, Kale, and Chorizo Soup	165	8
Carrot Soup with Ginger Essence	121	6
Cauliflower Vichyssoise with Chive Cream	73	4
Chilled Spring Pea Soup	144	2
"Cream" of Swiss Chard	138	5
Garlic Soup with Chicken and Cilantro	114	1
Iced Cucumber–Spearmint Soup	86	2
Red Lentil Soup with Coconut Milk and Scallions	212	2
Roasted Beet and Orange "Latte"	159	2
Roasted Tomato–Pepper Gazpacho, Basil Oil	141	9
Sweet Potato–Rutabaga Soup with Bacon Crisps	159	5
Thick Fennel Soup with Spinach Pastina	105	1
Yellow Split Pea and Smoked Salmon Bisque	261	2
Zucchini Foam with Crab	81	1

SOUP ACCOMPANIMENTS

	Cal	Fat
Lemon-Poppy Wafers (each)	30	1
Parmesan Crisps (each)	35	1

FIRST COURSES

COLD

	Cal	Fat
1-2-3 Tomato Salad with Ricotta Salata and Dill*	128	5
A Trio of Roasted Peppers and Radish Sprouts, Creamy Feta Dressing	100	4
Beet "Carpaccio," Lemony Tonnato Sauce	165	7
Chilled Oysters, Sake-Shallot Mignonette	133	2
Eggplant and Roasted Pepper Terrine	158	11
Endive Leaves and "Endive Marmalade," White Balsamic Vinaigrette	137	11
Fancy Mixed Greens, Tangerine Vinaigrette	135	11
Honeydew "Carpaccio" with Air-Dried Beef and Asiago	152	5
Jean-Georges' Leek Terrine with Caviar	214	5
Julienned Beefsteak Tomato Salad, Watercress Oil	149	11
Jumbo Shrimp on the Half Shell, "8-Vegetable" Granita	134	2
"Lamb's-Quarters" Lettuce and Pear Salad, Stilton Dressing	165	9
Plum Tomato Salad with Bocconcini and Tomato Frappè	130	7

(Analysis for this recipe is done with feta cheese; ricotta salata not available.)

	Cal	Fat
Poached Salmon, Cilantro-Yogurt Sauce	165	6

Six Dips for Crudités and Steamed Vegetables (*per tablespoon*):

	Cal	Fat
Beetroot-Yogurt	8	1
Cucumber-Scallion	15	1
Goat Cheese–Cilantro	34	3
Red Pepper and Eggplant "Ketchup"	12	0
Roquefort-Basil	19	1
Yogurt-Tahini	18	1
Smoked Salmon with Wasabi Cream	134	9
Wasabi Clams with Pickled Ginger	119	1
Yogurt Cheese "Caprese," Sun-Dried Tomatoes and Basil	96	3

ROOM-TEMPERATURE AND WARM

	Cal	Fat
Arugula and Warm Cherry Tomato Salad	133	9
Parmesan-Crusted Asparagus, Poached Egg	165	9
Roasted Asparagus and Orange Salad, Asparagus "Fettuccine"	148	7
Sautéed Shrimp in Corn-Milk Sauce	165	6
Seared Smoked Salmon, Cucumbers Pressé	149	9
Wilted Fennel and Grape Tomato Salad, Tomato Dressing	160	11

MAIN COURSES

	Cal	Fat
Baked Arctic Char with Dill and Vermouth	300	10
Baked Fennel Parmigiana	270	8
Basil-Stuffed Swordfish	340	20
Bay-Steamed Halibut with Lemon Oil	332	14
Bluefish under a Brick, Whole-Poached Scallions	284	9
Boeuf à la Ficelle with Shiitakes and Ginger	350	20
Brined Pork Loin with Orange-Chipotle Jus	330	12
Chicken and Leeks in Double-Strength Sherry Consommé	328	7
Chicken Chaud Froid with Yogurt-Lime Glaze	312	6
Chicken Velvet Salad	331	12
Chilean Sea Bass on Braised Savoy Cabbage	350	17
Cold Poached Chicken, Avocado and Mango Mousseline	346	12
Cumin-Crusted Lamb with Apricots	346	11
Duck Magret with Roasted Red Onions and Pomegranate Molasses	350	12
Lacquered Salmon, Pineapple-Soy Reduction	318	10
Lamb Chops Provençal	343	16
Layered Flounder and Smoked Salmon	333	6
Lemon Sole in Tomato and Preserved Lemon Sauce	286	3
Lemon-Thyme Roast Chicken with Pan Juices	350	20
Miso-Glazed Grouper, Japanese-Style	289	4
Next Wave Tuna Salad: Tartare and Seared	346	16
Orecchiette with Broccoli, Broccoli-Butter Sauce	350	9

	Cal	Fat
Strawberry-Coconut Shake	108	3
Tropical Soy Frullato	148	3
Watermelon Splash	95	0

HOT

	Cal	Fat
Chamomile Tea with Lavender	15	0
Ginseng Tea with Maple-Ginger Essence	45	0
Green Apple Tisane with Tarragon	60	0
Immune Tea	10	0
Laughing "Milk"	132	6
Lemon Balm Soother	51	0
"Penicillin"	40	1
Spiced "Coffee"	38	0
Strawberry-Basil Elixir	55	0
White "Tea"	68	0
Wise Woman Sage Tea	38	0

FRUITS AND DESSERTS

COLD FRUITS

	Cal	Fat
1-2-3 Fruit Soup	116	0
"Canary" Soup with Melon Balls, Mint, and Lime Oil	80	1
Cantaloupe and Raspberries, Melba Sauce and Melon Ribbons	158	0
Crown of Figs and Raspberries, Rock Sugar and Fig Coulis	288	0
Fresh Apricots in Cinnamon Syrup	115	0
Fresh Blueberries and Blueberry Compote, Lemon "Custard"	165	2
Mangoes and Blackberries, Blackberry Coulis	215	0
Melon au Porto	155	0
Peaches in Peach Schnapps with Basil	123	0
Pineapple Shingles with Caramel, Pistachio Dust	165	4
Pink Grapefruit in Guava Nectar, Candied Violets	212	0
Poached Seckel Pears, Maple-Cardamom Syrup	165	0
Prunes and Chocolate, Port Wine Sauce	284	5
Raspberry-Honey Fool	223	0
Rosemary-Poached Pears "Vino Cotto"	218	0
Watermelon "Carpaccio" with White Chocolate	165	7
Yogurt "Cheese" Terrine with Giant Strawberries, Pineapple Syrup	158	0

FRUITS AND SORBETS

	Cal	Fat
Anjou Pears and Grappa, Pear Granita	235	0
granita only	83	0
Baked Sabra Oranges, Chocolate-Orange Sorbet	260	0
sorbet only	60	0
Frosted Lemons with Yogurt Gelato	151	1
Poached Pineapple in Red Honey Syrup, Rose Hips Sorbet	204	0
sorbet only	90	0
Red and White Cherry Soup with Star Anise, Cherry Ice		
soup	138	0
ice	49	0
Strawberry-Ginger Sorbet, Macerated Berries, and Ginger Chips	165	0
sorbet only	78	0
Turkish Apricots with Tarragon, Almond Sorbetto	231	0
sorbet only	78	0

WARM FRUITS

	Cal	Fat
Baked Plums with Walnut Crunch, Red Plum Sauce	165	9
Cider-Poached Apples, Cider Syrup, and Swirls of Cream	237	5
Orange Gratin with Pineapple-Orange Sabayon	205	5
Warm Rhubarb Compote, Vanilla Yogurt Timbale	162	1

CAKES AND COOKIES

	Cal	Fat
A Simple Vanilla Gâteau	222	3
Biscottini (each)	62	1
Chocolate Mousse Sponge	164	11
Cinnamon-Chocolate Ciambella	159	7
Cinnamon-Sugar Crisps (each)	33	1
Cocoa Meringues (each)	18	0
French Walnut Torte	165	11

FRUIT AND CHEESE

	Cal	Fat
Brie and Seckel Pear, Dried Figs	164	8
Bosc Pears and Parmigiano-Reggiano, Melon Liqueur	114	5
Cabrales Cheese with Roasted Grapes	165	8
Cantaloupe with Manchego and Honey	133	7
Stilton Cheese and Roasted Lady Apples, Port Syrup	165	6
Watermelon, Feta, and Mint	115	7

acknowledgments

To my circle of wise women: my beautiful mother, Marion Gold; Helen Kimmel, MS, RD, nutritionist extraordinaire; Dale Glasser Bellisfield, RN, CH, clinical herbalist; Amy Berkowitz, RN; Dr. Barbara Levine, RD, PhD; Fern Gale Estrow, MS, RD, CDN; Carol Guber, MS; Dr. Judy Nelson; Gail Gold; Paige Sarlin; Bea Lewis; Phyllis Feder; Marcy Blum; Susy Davidson; Rona Jaffe; Ann Feld; Fern Berman; Carol Levy; Jan Fitzpatrick; Laura Lehrman; Nancy Arum; Barbara Cohen; Audrey Appleby; Diana Carulli Dunlap; Iris Carulli; Nancy Arum; Phyllis Glazer; Robin Zucker; Sally-Jo O'Brien, who is always there for me; Marion Wiener, who helped test recipes; Margarette Adams, food stylist; Judy Rundel, my wine advisor; Erica Marcus, who first blessed this project and guided me so intelligently; Amanda Wilson, who designed this book so beautifully; and to Leslie Stoker, the finest and wisest woman in publishing.

To my dad, Bill Gold; my brother, Dr. Leon Gold; my son, Jeremy Whiteman; Arthur Schwartz; Bob Harned; Steve North; Marc Summers; Francesco de'Rogati; Dennis Sweeney; Ben Feder; Eddie Schoenfeld; "Thor," a.k.a. Paul Friedman, my personal trainer; and to the late, beloved Mike Hall.

Special thanks to *everyone* at Stewart, Tabori & Chang. Brava to Anita Calero, for her little photographic masterpieces.

Much love to Michael Whiteman, the smartest man I know. Thanks for our beautiful life together.

biographical information

Helen Kimmel, MS, RD is a Registered Dietitian, Certified Nutritionist and the founder of Foodworks, Inc., a culinary and nutrition consulting firm. She began her career as the staff nutritionist at the legendary Rainbow Room, helping develop "Evergreen," a spa program for members of the Rockefeller Center Luncheon Club. As a nutrition consultant, her many projects include *A Feast for the Heart,* by W. Gelber (Little, Brown & Co.), Rozanne Gold's 1-2-3 series, *Reader's Digest Cookbooks,* and *Kosher Gourmet Magazine.* Helen has been featured on CNN and has lectured for Cornell University and The American Heart Association. An accomplished culinary instructor, Helen organizes healthy cooking classes for diabetics, heart, and Alzheimer patients. She lives and cooks in New Jersey with her husband and two children.

Dale Bellisfield, RN, CH is an honors graduate Registered Nurse and a Clinical Herbalist. She has more than ten years of education and training, in several traditions of herbal medicine, under some of the most renowned herbalists in the country. She is currently working as an herbalist in conjunction with physicians at Kessler Institute for Rehabilitation and at Hackensack Medical Center's new holistic Center for Health and Healing in New Jersey, as well as at Greyston, an HIV treatment center in Yonkers, NY. She teaches and lectures extensively in the New York/New Jersey area, where she also maintains a private practice. Her company, The Fertile Hand Inc., offers exclusive organic products for the body, both inside and out. She is married, has a teen-age daughter, and lives in New Jersey.

bibliography

Balch, P. and J., *Prescription for Dietary Wellness,* 64, Avery Publishing, NY, 1992.

Bianchini, F., *The Complete Book of Fruits and Vegetables,* Crown Publishers, NY, 1976.

Colbin, A., *Food and Healing,* 45, 202–203, Ballantine Books, NY, 1986.

Davidson, A., *The Oxford Companion to Food,* Oxford University Press, NY, 1999.

Duke, J., *The Green Pharmacy,* 249–250, St. Martin's Press, NY, 1997.

Dunne, L., *Nutrition Almanac,* 247–249, 268–307, McGraw-Hill, NY, 1990.

Finkel, Dr. H., *In Vino Sanitas?,* Society of Wine Educators, Inc., MD, 1998.

Gershoff, S., *The Tufts University Guide to Total Nutrition,* HarperCollins Publishers, NY, 1996.

Health Magazine, *The Healing Power of Superfoods,* Time Inc. Health, San Francisco, 1999.

Hess, L. H. D. and A. E. Hunt, Hess and Hunt, Inc. *Review of Dietetics,* Hess and Hunt, Inc. Nutrition Communications, Winnetka, 1992.

Hobbs, C., *Medicinal Mushrooms,* 38–40, 125–138, Botanica Press, CA, 1995.

Jensen, B., *Foods That Heal,* 159–162, 199–200, 218–219, Avery Publishing, NY, 1993.

Lawless, J., *The Illustrated Encyclopedia of Essential Oils,* 117, Barnes and Noble Books, NY, 1995.

Leung, A., *Chinese Healing Foods and Herbs,* 146–149, AYSL Corp., NJ, 1984.

Lust, J., *The Herb Book,* 164, 377, Bantam Books, NY, 1974.

Lyman, Ph.D., B., *A Psychology of Food,* Van Nostrand Reinhold, NY, 1989.

Margen, M.D., S., University of California at Berkeley, *The Wellness Encyclopedia of Food and Nutrition,* REBUS Random House, NY, 1992.

Mortimore, D. *The Complete Illustrated Guide to Nutritional Healing,* 34–41, Barnes and Noble Books, NY, 1998.

Ratsch, C., *Plants of Love,* 70, 118–123, Ten Speed Press, CA, 1997.

Richardson, J., *The Little Herb Encyclopedia: The Handbook of Nature's Remedies for a Healthier Life,* Woodland Health Books, UT, 1995.

Robinson, J., *The Oxford Companion to Wine,* Oxford University Press, 1994.

Sizer, F. and Whitney, E. *Nutrition Concepts and Controversies,* Wadsworth/Thomson Learning, Belmont, CA 2000

Turner, L., *Meals That Heal,* 17–76, Healing Arts Press, VT, 1996.

Tyler, V. E., *The Honest Herbal,* Pharmaceutical Products Press, NY, 1993.

USDA, *Composition of Foods,* Agriculture Handbook, numbers 8–17, USDA, Washington, 1989.

Van Straten, M., *Healing Foods,* 61–121, 124–129, Welcome Rain, NY, 1997.

Weil, Dr. A., *Natural Health, Natural Medicine,* Houghton Mifflin, NY, 1998

Weil, Dr. A., *Eating Well for Optimum Health,* Alfred A. Knopf, NY, 2000

Weiss, S., ed., et al., *Foods That Harm, Foods That Heal,* 330, Reader's Digest Association, NY, 1997.

Williams, S., *Essentials of Nutrition and Diet Therapy,* 101–164, Mosby, MO, 1994.

Winston, D., *Course Curriculum Notes,* Herbal Therapeutics School of Botanical Medicine, NJ, 1994–1996.

Wood, R., *The Whole Foods Encyclopedia,* Penguin Books, New York, 1999.

World Cancer Research Fund, *Food, Nutrition and the Prevention of Cancer: A Global Perspective,* American Institute for Cancer Research, Washington, D.C., 1997

Yeager, S., *Prevention's New Foods for Healing,* Rodale Press, Inc., Emmaus, PA, 1998.

metric conversion

Weight Equivalents

The metric weights given in this chart are not exact equivalents, but have been rounded up or down slightly to make measuring easier.

Avoirdupois	Metric
¼ oz	7 g
½ oz	15 g
1 oz	30 g
2 oz	60 g
3 oz	90 g
4 oz	115 g
5 oz	150 g
6 oz	175 g
7 oz	200 g
8 oz (½ lb)	225 g
9 oz	250 g
10 oz	300 g
11 oz	325 g
12 oz	350 g
13 oz	375 g
14 oz	400 g
15 oz	425 g
16 oz (1 lb)	450 g
1½ lb	750 g
2 lb	900 g
2¼ lb	1 kg
3 lb	1.4 kg
4 lb	1.8 kg

Volume Equivalents

These are not exact equivalents for American cups and spoons, but have been rounded up or down slightly to make measuring easier.

American	Metric	Imperial
¼ t	1.2 ml	
½ t	2.5 ml	
1 t	5.0 ml	
½ T (1.5 t)	7.5 ml	
1 T (3 t)	15 ml	
¼ cup (4 T)	60 ml	2 fl oz
⅓ cup (5 T)	75 ml	2½ fl oz
½ cup (8 T)	125 ml	4 fl oz
⅔ cup (10 T)	150 ml	5 fl oz
¾ cup (12 T)	175 ml	6 fl oz
1 cup (16 T)	250 ml	8 fl oz
1¼ cups	300 ml	10 fl oz (½ pt)
1½ cups	350 ml	12 fl oz
2 cups (1 pint)	500 ml	16 fl oz
2½ cups	625 ml	20 fl oz (1 pint)
1 quart	1 liter	32 fl oz

Oven Temperature Equivalents

Oven	F	C	Gas Mark
Very cool	250-275	130-140	½-1
Cool	300	150	2
Warm	325	170	3
Moderate	350	180	4
Moderately hot	375	190	5
	400	200	6
Hot	425	220	7
	450	230	8
Very hot	475	250	9

index

(Page mumbers in *italic* refer to illustrations).

hilled Spring Pea Soup • Cauliflower Vichyssoise with Chive Cream • Brocco
ucumber-Spearmint Soup • Carrot Soup with Ginger Essence • Yellow Split P
ntil Soup with Coconut Milk and Scallions • Sweet Potato–Rutabaga Soup w
range "Latte" • "Cream" of Swiss Chard • Roasted Tomato–Pepper Gazpacho, Bas
udités and Steamed Vegetables • Beetroot-Yogurt • Roquefort-Basil • Red Pepper
oneydew "Carpaccio" with Air-Dried Beef and Asiago • Chilled Oysters, Sake-Shallo
aviar • Fancy Mixed Greens, Tangerine Vinaigrette • Plum Tomato Salad with Bocc
asabi Clams with Pickled Ginger • A Trio of Roasted Peppers and Radish Sprouts,
eet "Carpaccio," Lemony Tonnato Sauce • Eggplant and Roasted Pepper Terrin
armalade," White Balsamic Vinaigrette • Yogurt Cheese "Caprese," Sun-Dried To
mato Salad, Watercress Oil • Arugula and Warm Cherry Tomato Salad • Seare
gg • Roasted Asparagus and Orange Salad, Asparagus "Fettuccine" • Wilte
ilk Sauce • Polenta Tart with Melted Tomatoes and Smoked Mozzarella •
recchiette with Broccoli, Broccoli-Butter Sauce • Penne with Zucchini, Zuc
moky Shrimp with Steamed Bok Choy and Oyster Sauce • Salmon Arrosto
alibut with Lemon Oil • Basil-Stuffed Swordfish • Seared Swordfish with Fr
tic Char with Dill and Vermouth • Chilean Sea Bass on Braised Savoy Ca
oached Scallions • Sautéed Cod with Asparagus, Asparagus Veloutè • Stea
mon Sole in Tomato and Preserved Lemon Sauce • Miso-Glazed Grouper, Ja
hicken with Pan Juices • Chicken Velvet Salad • Chicken and Leeks in Do
ousseline • Tandoori Chicken on the Bone • Sautéed Chicken Breasts wit
th Sumac and Shallots • Turkey Salad with Grape Tomatoes and Zucchini, Z
Duck Magret with Roasted Red Onions and Pomegranate Molasses • Brine
osemary • Potted Leeks and Corned Beef in Riesling • Cumin-Crusted Lam
celle with Shiitakes and Ginger • Grated Carrot–Citrus Salad • Yellow Tomato Sals